"In today's fast-paced world, nothing stays static for long. Jolt! provides smart ideas on how to embrace change in a tangible and powerful way."
—DAN LIN, PRODUCER OF *SHERLOCK HOLMES* I & 2
AND EXECUTIVE PRODUCER OF *TERMINATOR SALVATION*

"The world has changed and nothing will ever be the same again. Most people have reacted by hunkering down and settling into survival mode. In *Jolt!*, Phil Cooke brilliantly shows us that we were created for something far greater. We don't have to have life dictated to us. We can rise above the chaos and stay ahead of the curve."
—STEVEN FURTICK, LEAD PASTOR, ELEVATION
CHURCH AND AUTHOR OF *SUN STAND STILL*

"Today's ever-changing and fast paced world can be overwhelming. *Jolt!* offers unique and inspiring solutions to problems that arise in the busy and chaotic times we live in. It will equip you with the tools to move forward in life with new passion and determination."
—JOYCE MEYER, BIBLE TEACHER
AND BEST-SELLING AUTHOR

"When I created the nationwide "Get Motivated Seminars," one of my driving passions was to help professionals understand today's rapidly changing business world. *Jolt!* is a roadmap for understanding those changes. If you're serious about success, this is the book I recommend."
—PETER LOWE, FOUNDER OF
THE GET MOTIVATED SEMINARS

ONE
B1G
THING

OTHER BOOKS BY PHIL COOKE:

Jolt: Get the Jump on a World That's Constantly Changing

Branding Faith: Why Some Churches and Non-profits Impact the Culture and Others Don't

The Last TV Evangelist: Why the Next Generation Couldn't Care Less About Religious Media

ONE
B1G
THING

Discovering What You Were Born to Do

PHIL COOKE

THOMAS NELSON
Since 1798

NASHVILLE   DALLAS   MEXICO CITY   RIO DE JANEIRO

To my incredible daughters,
Kelsey and Bailey

Published in Nashville, Tennessee, by Thomas Nelson. Thomas Nelson is a registered trademark of Thomas Nelson, Inc.

Scripture quotations marked KJV are from the Holy Bible, King James Version.

Thomas Nelson, Inc., titles may be purchased in bulk for educational, business, fund-raising, or sales promotional use. For information, please e-mail SpecialMarkets@ThomasNelson.com.

ISBN-13: 978-1-40027-483-3 (IE)

Library of Congress Cataloging-in-Publication Data

Cooke, Phil, 1954-
  One big thing : discovering what you were born to do / Phil Cooke.
    p. cm.
  Includes bibliographical references and index.
  ISBN 978-1-59555-484-0
  1. Self-actualization (Psychology) 2. Self-realization. 3. Meaninglessness (Philosophy) I. Title.
  BF637.S4C657 2012
  158.1--dc23

                          2012002924

Printed in the United States of America

12 13 14 15 16 QG 6 5 4 3 2 1

CURLY: *Do you know what the secret of life is?*
[holds up one finger]
This.
MITCH: *Your finger?*
CURLY: *One thing. Just one thing. You stick
to that and the rest don't mean s***.*
MITCH: *But what is the "one thing"?*
CURLY: *That's what you have to find out.*

—From the movie *City Slickers*

CONTENTS

Contents

Introduction

THE BIG QUESTIONS

This one thing I do . . .

—THE APOSTLE PAUL (PHILIPPIANS 3:13 KJV)

A ship is safe in harbor, but that's not what ships are for.

—WILLIAM SHEDD, NINETEENTH-CENTURY AMERICAN THEOLOGIAN

Y ou are facing two big questions:

QUESTION 1: WHAT AM I SUPPOSED TO DO WITH MY LIFE?

I believe it's a heartfelt question millions ask on a daily basis. Why am I here? What am I supposed to accomplish? What was I born to do?

In one form or another, it's the Big Question that paralyzes people's futures, freezes their momentum, and stalls their promise. It keeps millions of people from fulfilling their potential and making a difference with their lives. I speak at conferences around the world, and afterward people literally line up to ask me the Big Question. In other situations, they pull me aside after business meetings, approach me through social media, or ask through a mutual friend.

The Big Question comes in many ways, but typically I'll hear something like: "Phil, I'm really unhappy at my job. But frankly, I don't know what I'm supposed to be doing with my life. I don't even know what I'm good at, so I'm not sure where to look or start."

Some actually feel guilty because while everyone else admires them or thinks they have it made, the truth is, they are really miserable.

That may sound like you.

You may be a college student, recent graduate, experienced businessperson, employee, housewife, or you may be unemployed and wondering why. Oddly enough, I've heard the Big Question from as many CEOs and business leaders as I've heard it from those at the bottom of the job ladder.

But that's not a surprise, because as you may have discovered, you can go through your entire working life, and still not really know what your purpose is, or what you were born to accomplish.

> *"Would you tell me, please, which way I ought to go from here?"*
>
> *"That depends a good deal on where you want to get to," said the Cat.*
>
> *"I don't much care where—" said Alice.*
>
> *"Then it doesn't matter which way you go," said the Cat.*

—Conversation between Alice and the Cheshire Cat, from *Alice's Adventures in Wonderland* by Lewis Carroll

» What could you be the best in the world at doing?

I love asking this question: *What could you be the best in the world at doing?* If you've met me in the last ten years, you've probably heard me ask it, and I usually push pretty hard for an answer. I'm not really looking for the best computer programmer, athletic coach, salesperson, or graphic designer in the world. I'm really trying to see what you feel is your greatest strength. Where you could compete. Where you stand out. What's your niche. What areas of your life are you most proud of?

Where could you be remarkable?

A few years ago, I shared a cab with the CEO of a successful medical supply company. He was in his mid-fifties, made a hefty salary, and led a very large company. But when I asked him this question, he was baffled. After a few uncomfortable minutes of consideration, he finally said: "Honestly, I have no idea. I went into this business on the recommendation of a friend. A member of our team happened to invent a best-selling medical device, and we all sort of rose to the top together. But why am I in this position? I really can't say. Do I find fulfillment here? Not really. It's a good salary, but at the end of the day, I'd have to admit that I have no idea if I'm actually doing what I was really put on the earth to accomplish."

My question bothered him enough that he quietly stared out the window of the cab for the rest of the trip to the airport, and except for a brief good-bye, he was lost in thought, and we never shared another word.

QUESTION 2: IN A HYPER-COMPETITIVE, CLUTTERED, AND DISTRACTED WORLD, HOW DO I GET NOTICED?

The second Big Question is, *How do I get noticed?* or *How do I get my voice heard?* Or even, *How do I get my dream project on the radar?*

Even if you have figured out your purpose—your One Big Thing—so what? You may be driven to tell that story or share that message. We all have dreams. But we struggle with connecting with the right person, circumstance, or situation to make that dream happen. After all, we live in a culture where ideas happen 24/7. New mobile apps pop up daily, more and more competition descends on Hollywood every year to make movies, self-publishing has exponentially increased the competition for book sales, and even in your office, someone's out for your job.

Whatever you do in life, you have a big target on your forehead, and there are millions of people out there taking aim.

**When you are not practicing, remember,
someone somewhere is practicing, and
when you meet him he will win.**
—Ed Macauley, basketball player

You might be an employee or leader with a great idea for the organization, a pastor with a book manuscript or ministry idea, a director or producer with a great film concept, or anyone else with an original idea burning a hole in your heart. You carry it like a child inside ready to be born.

But the problem is no one's listening.

You *know* it could work. You feel it in your bones. But the truth is, if no one's there to help you make it a reality, then what's the point? I meet "idea people" in Hollywood all the time. They have plenty of dreams, but no way of making them happen. As a result, they wander from party to party, event to event, conference to conference hoping to meet the *right person* to say, "Yes!" The kind of person who sees what they see and wants to help. (Hopefully without ripping them off in the process.)

>> **The intersection of those two questions
is what this book is about.**

I can't determine your purpose in life. That's something between you, your conscience, and God. But I can certainly point you in the right direction, and show you the questions you need to be asking on the journey.

I think they're the most important questions you can possibly ask: Why am I here? What was I born to accomplish? How do I make that purpose known to others? How do I get my message, idea, or story noticed?

Discovering that unique purpose is important, but in the twenty-first century, it takes more than just identifying that One Big Thing, or OBT. Today, if you're going to influence your family, company, community, or the world, you have to get it noticed. You may have a remarkable gift for inspiring people, but until you learn how to get that message heard, your impact will be small.

> **The mass of men lead lives of quiet desperation. What is called resignation is confirmed desperation.**
> **—Henry David Thoreau, philosopher and naturalist**

Ron Chernow's biography of George Washington (Penguin Press) tells the remarkable story of a leader who wasn't necessarily a brilliant military strategist but had a powerful and sharp eye for acting at the right moment. In both his career and his personal life, Washington had instincts that were usually right on target. As a result, he could turn defeat into victory and take advantage of other's mistakes; his extraordinary ability to lead and inspire his men overcame other areas of weakness. Washington's lessons have never become outdated. In fact, Andrew Roberts, reviewing the book for the *Wall Street Journal* stated that Washington's leadership techniques were as potent today as they were in the late eighteenth century.[1]

George Washington was a great leader because he knew himself and his purpose.

How about you? Do you know yourself and your purpose well enough to be ready when your moment of destiny arrives?

When writing *The Gathering Storm*, volume 1 of his history of the second World War, Winston Churchill said: "I felt as if I was walking with destiny, and that all my past life had been but a preparation for this hour and this trial."

When a great challenge arrives, that's no time to figure out your strengths, weaknesses, and purpose. By then it's too late to find out what you're made of. That's why discovering your One Big Thing right now is the key to preparing you for whatever awaits in your future.

MOST COLLEGES AREN'T HELPING US DISCOVER OUR PURPOSE

A significant percentage of the millions of students who fill graduate schools today are desperately searching for their one thing. But rather than help them discover the secret that could launch them into a successful and fulfilling life, many universities simply keep the addiction going—capitalizing on that need in order to keep tuition coming in and filling seats. Years ago, colleges and universities actually prepared men and women for a productive future. They weren't afraid to teach real workplace skills and back up that instruction with moral principles and values to help them make functional decisions in the battle of life.

But today, the powerful foundation of learning the West was built on through the centuries has crumbled in favor of more trendy subjects. Across the country, university curricula are filled with courses like multiculturalism, gender studies, and deconstruction of philosophy, the classics, or even eighteenth-century interior design. They offer courses that *appear* to fulfill a deeper purpose in life without actually offering that purpose.

**Some people get an education
without going to college; the rest
get it after they get out.**

—Mark Twain, author and humorist

It's one of the reasons film schools are bursting at the seams. In the least likely places you can imagine, the smallest university programs are offering a film or cinema studies department—in many cases without a qualified faculty, equipment, or actual connections to the industry. But it's in demand, so they create programs—sometimes, it appears, out of thin air. Are they actually helping these students?

It's doubtful.

As a result, tens of thousands of young film school graduates descend on Hollywood every year fighting for the scraps from the table from those truly driven and gifted at making films. The rest either sell real estate and call themselves "idea people" at parties, or simply go back and reenroll in graduate film studies programs and keep the cycle (and illusion) going.

Either way, they're not finding the real answers they're looking for.

As Pulitzer Prize–winning playwright and filmmaker David Mamet writes in his book *The Secret Knowledge: On the Dismantling of American Culture*: "Higher Education is selling an illusion: that a child of the well-to-do need not matriculate into the workforce—that mastery of a fungible skill is not necessary. Who does not know the thirty-year-old described by his parents as 'still searching for himself'? By forty, this person is, by his parents, generally not described at all, for to do so would be either to skirt or to employ the term 'bum.'"

I support higher education, and lecture at colleges and universities around the world. But while a great many university students are serious and tackle the difficult challenges of education, there are others simply taking the easy way out. And when it comes to helping us discover our purpose in life, I'm afraid that far too many colleges and universities have taken the easier road—the politically correct road. They've traded helping us discover our destiny for an endless parade of classes and courses celebrating the trivial.

IT'S NOT ABOUT TRENDS; IT'S ABOUT OUR LIVES

This quest is big. It's important. Finding the answer could redefine the way you live and what you accomplish with your life. We all know the thirty-year-old still "finding himself" that Mamet writes about. He tries a little of this and a little of that. Doesn't seem to stick with anything long. He lives with his mom so he doesn't feel the heat and financial pressure of real survival.

But at the other end of the spectrum, there are millions who are actually successful on the outside and yet miserable on the inside. The irony is that some of these financially prosperous men and women think they're helping the cause by giving to educational institutions that are actually undermining that search. Institutions that instead of planting a burning desire to impact the world are funneling students into fringe studies like the "underwater basket-weaving" courses we used to joke about.

**The real voyage of discovery lies
not in seeking new landscapes,
but in seeing with new eyes.**
—Marcel Proust, French novelist

Then again, there's you and me. Not a bum, not necessarily rich or even well off—just frustrated. Frustrated that we can't seem to find our niche. Can't find the burning passion that makes us want to leap out of bed in the morning. Can't find the thing that leaves us feeling like we matter. The One Big Thing that when finished for the day, we drop into a deep and satisfying sleep, knowing that we've done our best at what we were put on the earth to accomplish.

And if we're one of those who do know our purpose, how do we share that message with others? How do we get our work noticed? How do we get published, produced, created, or funded?

This is your life and it's ending one minute at a time.
—**Narrator, *Fight Club* (1999), from the novel by Chuck Palahniuk**

In the wonderful book *The Answer to How Is Yes*, Peter Block put it this way: "It is entirely possible to spend our days engaged in activities that work well for us and achieve our objectives, and still wonder whether we are really making a difference in the world. My premise is that this culture, and we as members of it, have yielded too easily to what is doable and practical and popular. In the process we have sacrificed the pursuit of what is in our hearts."

The journey you are beginning is immeasurably important. On the road ahead you'll encounter frustrations, obstacles, and even failures, but you'll have the knowledge that you're finally looking at the right map, and you're moving forward.

This book won't give you all the answers, but it will help you start asking the right questions.

> **What really matters is what you
> do with what you have.**
> —H. G. Wells, English author

As we start this journey together, there are a few important rules:

*First, understand that discovering your One Big
Thing isn't about your position in life, the size
of your bank account, or your current job.*

This quest is about something far bigger than a job, and it's a question that everyone, everywhere, needs to be asking. You may be unemployed and unfulfilled, or you may be a billionaire and just as unfulfilled. Either way, you'll be miserable until you understand your OBT. Status, bank accounts, or past achievements don't matter on the journey to discovering your purpose.

Second, it won't necessarily be easy.

In a self-help world, some people think all we need is the latest book about overcoming whatever obstacle we're facing. That's why the self-help sections of the bookstore are so packed. While this isn't a book about complicated theories, figuring out formulas, or deep research, finding your One Big Thing is a journey that requires commitment. It goes almost without saying that the answer isn't always obvious. I'm bringing this information to the table, but you need to bring your life experience, talents, gifts, and aspirations. Working together is the key, and this task isn't for sissies.

*Third, start looking at your life with
a new honesty and clarity.*

It's no secret that millions of people live in denial rather than doing the hard work of facing life with honesty. It's just so easy to justify and rationalize our failures rather than do the heavy lifting of facing our shortcomings and changing our lives.

Every year in Hollywood I attend film screenings of movies that cost millions to produce, and others with microbudgets that only cost hundreds. My wife and I watched a full-length feature film recently that cost just fifteen hundred dollars to produce, and it was pretty impressive. But that film only happened because of the time and commitment of a very creative and driven team—a team who honestly came to terms with their budget limitations but moved forward understanding that reality.

Great things aren't accomplished by people who live in denial, or refuse to face the truth. Your current circumstances aren't nearly as big a factor as you think. It's not about where you are, it's about where you're going. The point is that if you have passion, drive, and commitment—and will look at your life with honesty—almost anything could happen. In my work with global organizations I find that most have plenty of vision, but many haven't created the kind of original, innovative culture that can make that vision happen.

Finally, this isn't a how-to book. It's not a checklist of simple steps, because when it comes to the biggest questions of life, it takes a little wrestling. In the New Testament book of Philippians, the apostle Paul reminds us to "work out your own salvation with fear and trembling" (2:12). The hard work of finding your One Big Thing isn't much different. Don't expect "five easy steps" or "ten miracle keys" here—expect to think.

I'm not a researcher, I'm an observer. You'll see the word *I* a lot in this book—not because I'm an egomaniac, but because I'm reporting back from having been on this same journey. From producing media programming in more than forty countries to directing prime-time television, being a business partner in a production company that produced Super Bowl commercials, to advising non-profit and humanitarian organizations around the world, to being one of the few working producers in Hollywood with a PhD—I'm reporting from the front lines. I'm not a travel agent, who gives you a brochure, I'm a tour guide who's actually been there before. I've been through the same frustrations, obstacles, and victories, and I'm simply sharing what I've learned along the way.

» **Plenty of people want to change the world, but not enough want to change themselves.**

Standing in line for a recent film screening, someone handed me a promotional card, and on the front it had this quote: "Don't ask yourself what the world needs. Ask yourself what makes you come alive and go do that, because what the world needs is people who have come alive.—Howard Thurman"

I know leaders who have great vision but are miserable. Employees who labor under the pressure of their jobs until they nearly crack. Organizations that cultivate an atmosphere of fear and intimidation. They may have a great vision, but are they making a difference?

Hardly.

What is it that makes you come alive? What excites and empowers you?

What were you born to do, and how can you get that message out there?

Let's go find some answers.

Chapter One

WHO'S PAINTING THE PORTRAIT OF YOUR LIFE?

The Power of Intentional Living

Every painter paints himself.

—CÒSIMO DE' MEDICI, FLORENTINE STATESMAN

I was going to have cosmetic surgery until I noticed that the doctor's office was full of portraits by Picasso.

—RITA RUDNER, COMEDIAN

A great life doesn't happen by accident. My wife, Kathleen, and I are regular visitors to the Huntington Library, Gardens, and Art Collection in Pasadena, California. Founded by Henry and Arabella Huntington, it is housed in the large Beaux Arts mansion (designed by architect Myron Hunt) they built shortly after the turn of the twentieth century; the home was transformed into a museum after Henry's death in 1927. At the age of sixty Henry retired from his extensive business interests in order to devote time to his book and art collections and the landscaping of his six hundred–acre ranch on which the mansion stands in San Marino, near Pasadena.

Among other outstanding collections, the museum boasts an incredible hall of portraits called the Thornton Portrait Gallery. As I walked through the halls looking at the political, artistic, social, and military leaders featured in the portraits, I was gripped by a distinct sense of "intention" in their faces. These were leaders from another century who lived strategically and with purpose. They didn't leave much to chance when it came to ambition and career goals.

>> **Leaders of the nineteenth century were good at knowing their One Big Thing.**

Walking through that gallery I realized that one of the key reasons these men and women were great was because they had discovered the power of *focus*. In today's culture it might seem restrictive to guide a young man or woman from childhood into a career in law, politics, the military, or music. Certainly in those days the options for a woman or member of a minority were far more limited than today.

But in the vast majority of cases, their lives were "designed" by their parents or their station in life. Few fought it, because at the time that was simply the way life was lived. They were all focused on One Big Thing. They had serious ambition, and lived lives of intentionality. As I studied the paintings of military generals, architects, writers and artists, business and government leaders, I wondered about the place of ambition in my own life. What would have happened had I lived my life more *intentionally?*

» **What could have happened if I had discovered my one thing sooner?**

I wonder if today we've become the victims of a desire to just live life as it comes—to assume that whatever works out is the best path. Especially if you're a child of the '60s, living a random life sounds somewhat romantic, but real influence in the world doesn't come at random. It rarely happens by accident. My father was a preacher from the South and had little knowledge of applying strategy to the art of living. As a result, I was well into my adult life before I even considered career planning or anything close to it. And by then it was pretty late.

Plus, coming from the Christian tradition as I do, it was actually frowned upon to take charge of our own lives. "Wait upon the Lord" was a refrain I heard a million times in church. We were encouraged to "seek His will for our lives," and see where He took us.

Today I look back and realize just how naïve I was. While each of those phrases is true, they're not referring to avoiding the hard work of discovering our place in this world. Jesus was a strong advocate of understanding the signs of the times and building upon a strong foundation:

Therefore everyone who hears these words of mine and puts them into practice is like a wise man who built his house on the rock. The rain came down, the streams rose, and the winds blew and beat against that house; yet it did not fall, because it had its foundation on the rock. But everyone who hears these words of mine and does not put them into practice is like a foolish man who built his house on sand. The rain came down, the streams rose, and the winds blew and beat against that house, and it fell with a great crash. (Matthew 7:24–27 NIV)

Without living strategically, our life could become a catastrophe. Walking through the Huntington Library's portrait gallery these questions swirled around in my mind:

- *What if from an early age, my parents had been looking for areas in which I excelled?*
- *What if they had focused my education to take advantage of those areas?*
- *What if my father had encouraged me to pursue a specific career?*
- *And even if I had picked it myself later, what if I had been more serious?*
- *What if I had pursued my goals with more conviction?*

"Things may come to those who wait, but only the things left by those who hustle." I'm told that quote is attributed to Abraham Lincoln, but hasn't been officially confirmed or denied by historians. (Did President Lincoln actually use the word *hustle*?) But either way, I like it. In many circles today, *ambition* is an ugly word. But the truth is, what's wrong with it? As long as it's braced with humility, what's wrong with planning, thinking ahead, and the desire to achieve something significant with our time on earth?

To influence today's culture, we need to have the experience, credentials, and relationships that only come by strategic living. Walking through that museum and staring up at those powerful portraits, I realized that great leaders of the past didn't just take life as it came—they understood how to make life happen.

WHAT'S THE DIFFERENCE
BETWEEN A JOB AND A DREAM?

One of my closest friends from high school has never discovered his one thing, and lives a life of misery. He began college with great excitement, but dropped out because he eventually lost interest. At one point he thought he wanted to be an actor, so he came to Hollywood. After a few years of failure, he took a class and became a real estate agent, but didn't last long there. He married, but the stress of never finding the right job broke that relationship apart.

Today, in his mid-fifties, he's working at a local coffee shop. Every day he reads the want ads, every day he scans the Internet for get-rich-quick ideas, and every day despairs of finding a dream he could call his own.

He's always worked hard, but the difference between a job and a dream has never been more clear than in the life of my friend.

What about you?

Is it time to discover the difference between a job and a dream?

Is it time to start living with purpose, intention, and ambition?

Who's painting the portrait of your life?

Chapter Two

DO WE REALLY HAVE A DESTINY?

Life's Loaded Question

You can't wait for inspiration.
You have to go after it with a club.

—Jack London, novelist

If you don't know where you are going,
you'll end up some place else.

—Yogi Berra, baseball legend

The issue of destiny is a loaded question. Nearly everyone wants to believe in the concept. Atheists may believe that there's no God, no purpose, and no point to life, but it's pretty tough living that philosophy out in the day-to-day trenches. The idea of destiny gives us a reason to go on, motivation that our lives matter beyond PTA meetings, job reviews, and visits to the local coffee shop.

The Christian tradition teaches that God has a purpose and plan for our lives. Because of the sacrifice of Jesus Christ on the cross, we have a higher calling and a guide to help us navigate our way through this world and the next. And Christians have certainly run with the destiny theme. Pastors use the word in their sermon and book titles, and if you look up Christian conferences, you'll be amazed how many use *destiny* in their title. There are Destiny conferences, Living Out Your Destiny conferences, Discovering Your Destiny conferences, Weekend of Destiny conferences, Women of Destiny conferences, the Affecting Destiny conferences, Spring Forth Destiny conferences, and I could go on and on. (Don't believe me? Just go online and search "destiny conference.")

Non-Christian traditions are no different. I was teaching in India recently and met a group of Hindu scholars discussing their own views about destiny. As I write this, the TV news is reporting the thousands of spiritualists and New Agers meeting at Stonehenge to welcome the summer solstice. The topic of discussion?

What does Stonehenge have to do with our destiny?

Religious or not, most people want to believe they have a purpose for living and would find it enormously difficult to go on without that knowledge.

So the question remains: *Do we have a destiny, and is it possible to discover it?*

I seriously doubt if we have a locked down, concrete, unchanging destiny we were born to accomplish. Destiny isn't a task. It's not an end point. It's not something you can check off a to-do list. In fact, that's where most people go wrong, and why so many attend destiny conferences, buy destiny books, and hear famous teachers speak on finding their destiny.

And why so many end up frustrated and unhappy.

» Your destiny is a moving target.

An unexpected divorce doesn't derail your destiny. The soldier who lost his legs in battle hasn't lost his destiny. Bankruptcy can't undermine your destiny.

Your destiny is a moving target, and that's why I prefer to use the word *purpose* or, as you've seen, your One Big Thing. Your purpose is bigger than any obstacle like physical limitations, financial circumstances, being fired, or other failures. Nothing can change the fact that you have a unique reason for being here, and there's still time for it to play out.

PURPOSE CAN BE REVEALED IN THREE IMPORTANT WAYS

First, in my experience, a handful of people have known it all their lives.

From a young age, it seems they've always known what they were born to accomplish and have pursued it with passion. I've met writers who have remarkable manuscripts they wrote as children; pastors who, at eight years old, stood on stools to preach to other kids in the neighborhood; and we've all met the whizkid who ran his lemonade stand like it was Walmart, while we stood by helpless with our cardboard box and plastic cups.

You're not one of these people because you're reading this book. They never think about discovering their purpose because it's all they've ever known. It's easy to be envious of these men and women because they've spent their lives focusing on the calling, and not having to anguish over which calling it might be.

A second group discovers their One Big Thing in a moment of epiphany.

Dictionary.com defines *epiphany* as "a sudden, intuitive perception of or insight into the reality or essential meaning of something, usually initiated by some simple, homely, or commonplace occurrence or experience."

In other words—a moment of revelation. The clouds part, the sun shines, and the angelic choir sings. I've heard thousands of stories of people who experienced this kind of moment—usually while in the act of *doing something*. I've discovered that most people experience that insight in the process of *action*. Few One Big Thing revelations come while sitting on the sofa watching *The Simpsons*. (That's not to say it couldn't happen.)

By the way—when I say *revelation* I'm not necessarily referring to some mystical, spooky, or spiritual experience. Very often a revelation is simply putting the pieces together. It's the moment when everything about your life makes sense and you suddenly see what you're supposed to be doing.

It's the "aha!" or "eureka!" moment.

Keep in mind that revelations come in all sizes and relate to all kinds of issues—most of which are not related to your OBT. I had a minor revelation this morning working on this book. I was unhappy with a section of the manuscript, but when I cut and pasted the section into another chapter, it suddenly all made sense. A chapter that I had been struggling with now works, and I only realized it the moment I hit paste and saw that section in context.

Hopefully these moments happen to you all the time:

- *The right person joins your team at the office and suddenly you're firing on all cylinders.*
- *Your child has a breakthrough in school that you never expected.*
- *You finally "get it" after staying up late to research the new project at work.*
- *Sitting in church, the pastor makes a statement that completely changes the way you look at a particular issue.*
- *Moving a single chair in your living room transforms the look and feel of your home.*
- *You finally understand what makes your spouse tick. (Okay—that was a stretch.)*

These are important and can sometimes make or break careers and relationships. But don't get them confused with the really big revelation about what you were born to accomplish. The moment when you discover your One Big Thing.

Finally, the third (and largest) group in my experience are the rest of us who discover our OBT through a much longer and progressive experience.

Rather than an explosive "aha!" moment, we find bits and pieces along the trail—take a few wrong turns in the process—and eventually start piecing together the puzzle of our lives.

This is the team I'm on, and chances are this is you as well.

I would have loved to have discovered my one thing as a young man and, like those leaders in the portrait gallery at the Huntington Library, pursued it with passion, conviction, and intention. But because I had no encouragement, training, or coaching, I wandered down many blind alleys and spent many years wondering if there was any purpose at all.

The list of things I was pursuing grew longer and longer—and trust me, I was serious about each one:

- *I thought about being a piano player, and made extra money in college playing at restaurants and clubs around town.*
- *I wanted to be an astronaut, and found a local congressman to vouch for my application to the Air Force Academy.*
- *I wanted to be an athlete and received multiple college sports scholarships.*
- *I did a short stint doing some pretty amateurish magic shows.*
- *I even have a drawer full of my unproduced screenplays, and an unpublished novel.*

So these and other attempts weren't passing fancies. I was committed, but never fulfilled. As a result, the more I searched the more frustrated I became.

It took me years before I started noticing the connections, honestly facing up to what I was *actually* good at doing versus what I *wanted* to do, and then finally embracing the way I was wired. Like picking up signs on a trail, things eventually began to make sense.

DESTINY WANTS TO BE PURSUED

Is there such a thing as destiny?

I think so, but we've spent too much time looking to the idea of destiny as a quick fix, a get-rich scheme, or a stopping point. We think we'll attend a conference and our destiny will be revealed to us during a workshop or seminar. We hope that it will descend out of the sky or someone will reveal it to us—for only a $49 conference fee.

Destiny wants to be pursued. It wants to be discovered. Why? Because it's in the journey we learn to understand and value what it means.

> **Destiny is not a matter of chance; but a matter of choice. It is not a thing to be waited for, it is a thing to be achieved.**
> **—William Jennings Bryan, politician**

Sometimes I meet people who always knew their One Big Thing, and you know what they struggle with? *I wonder if . . . ?* They wonder what their life might have been like had they pursued another path, or made another decision. They know they're doing exactly what they should be doing—and are perfectly satisfied—but late at night when nobody's watching, they fantasize about something else they might have done.

The successful Broadway singer wonders what it would have been like teaching music in high school.

The high-powered CEO wonders what it would have been like to run a small bookstore.

The powerful politician thinks about the days when she was interning at that social service agency downtown.

But you and I know better. We who have tried all those things, hit the dead ends, and slammed against our share of walls don't fantasize about other options because we've already experienced the obstacles. As we close in on our OBT, we can *focus*—undistracted by what might have been—because we know it already *was*.

What are your passions? Do you hide them under a bushel? Instead, tell the world that you love cooking, hockey, NASCAR, or—whatever it is—because pursuing your passions makes you more interesting, and interesting people are enchanting.
—**Guy Kawasaki, author of *Enchantment: The Art of Changing Hearts, Minds, and Actions***

We have a destiny. We have a purpose. We have one important thing. But it only comes with coaxing, work, and action. You're here because you haven't given up. You are determined to find the answer.

That determination alone may make the biggest difference.

Chapter Three

WHY ONE BIG THING?

Living in a Culture of Distraction

*We live in an age of wild media clutter, and big ideas
are more difficult to communicate than ever before.*

—DAVID DROGA, ADVERTISING AGENCY CHAIRMAN

Work is hard. Distractions are plentiful. And time is short.

—ADAM HOCHSCHILD, AUTHOR AND JOURNALIST

I've spent most of my life consulting for and advising large organizations, and one of the most common problems I encounter is that they're actually doing great things—*just too many of them*. In most cases, even the most successful organizations struggle because over the years they've been pulled in far too many directions.

Perhaps ten years ago a company decided to start a new product division, or a church launched a school, or a nonprofit developed a handful of new ideas and initiatives. Sure, they sounded good at the time, and were probably pretty effective for a while. But over the years, like barnacles on a ship, they start to slow the organization down to a crawl.

Not to mention deplete the bank account.

Sound like your life? How often have we said yes to things that sounded good at the time, only to discover they began dragging us down later? Like the barnacles, each of those commitments slows down our momentum and keeps us from accomplishing our dreams.

One of my favorite quotes is attributed to the brilliant artist Michelangelo. When an admirer asked him how he sculpted such wonderful statues, he replied that he didn't carve statues, he just removed the excess stone so the angel inside could be revealed.

A lot of what I do with organizations is to remove the excess stone. Typically, after years and sometimes decades, things—even good things—add up, and before long, they've become a completely different organization. They've wandered from their original calling, expertise, or brand, and customers or donors don't even recognize them anymore.

These frustrated organizations are a mile wide and an inch deep. They do a lot of things, but aren't extraordinary at any of them. The problem with cutting back is that they're very often *good* things. And most leaders find it difficult to cut these programs, divisions, or outreaches back (just look at the federal government). But the truth is, unless they can face the music and refocus, it will all eventually tumble like a house of cards.

My advice to these clients—and my advice to you—is the same: Step back and look at all that you're doing. What are you doing well and what not so well? What excites you and what doesn't? What reflects your genuine calling, expertise, and brand, and what doesn't? What will actually take you into the future? What could you potentially be the best in your field at accomplishing?

If it doesn't—like Michelangelo, start removing the excess stone. It's really about focusing *less* on what other people think is important, and *more* on what you were actually created to accomplish.

THE BREAD PLATE LADY

Recently, Kathleen and I spent the weekend in London, returning from a film project in Europe. If we're in London on a weekend, we always head out to Notting Hill for the Portobello Road street market. It's an incredible experience, and even in the dead of winter, it was packed with shoppers looking over the antiques, jewelry, rare books, clothes, and other wonderful stuff. Most of the stalls sold a variety of items, and I'm personally fascinated by the rare book dealers.

Toward the end of the day, we came upon a sweet little old lady in one of the smallest stalls who sold only two things: antique bread plates and their matching bread knives. The British apparently call them "bread plates" but we Americans call them cutting boards—although the British versions are shaped like a plate and beautifully carved.

Kathleen noticed a couple of plates from the mid-nineteenth century, and while she was looking at the collection, I struck up a conversation with the woman. I discovered she was in her eighties and had been selling antique bread plates for about forty-seven years. Since most of the sellers at the market sold a variety of antiques and other items, I asked her: "Why just this one thing? Why only bread plates?" She replied that forty-seven years ago she wanted a way to stand out and get noticed. She realized so many other stalls sold everything imaginable, so she decided she would focus.

>> **She didn't want to be lost in the clutter.**

She loved cooking and was fascinated by rare bread plates, so after much thinking, she decided that would be her focus. Now, all these years later, she's still at it, and it seemed like everyone at the market knew her as the "bread plate lady." She sells one thing and does it very well. That very nice grandmother had never been trained in marketing, and as far as she was concerned, branding was something done to a cow. But she instinctively understood how to cut through the clutter and get noticed in a crowd of competition.

Other shops at the market had some bread plates, but nothing like her collection. By focusing all her time and energy on one thing, she owned that niche, and was sought after by people seeking that particular item.

The questions are: Are you going to continue trying a little of this and a little of that? Being unremarkable at a lot of things? Getting lost in the clutter? Or are you going to find out what your One Big Thing is, let go of everything else, and pursue that with all your passion?

When I originally wrote the story of the bread plate lady on my blog at philcooke.com, I had a number of people who pushed back. Some people responded that they're good at a lot of things and couldn't possibly limit themselves to a single pursuit. In fact, the word *limit* is used frequently to argue against the idea of focusing our talent and passion in the pursuit of One Big Thing.

I understand where they're coming from. I play the piano, I'm fascinated by magic and magicians, I love history—especially the Revolutionary War period and the nineteenth-century age of discovery—I have a PhD in theology, my work is focused on filmmaking and TV production, I write books, I'm a professional speaker, I teach, snow ski, and the list goes on and on. I'm a passionate learner, and so I'm interested in a wide variety of subjects and issues.

The last thing in the world I would ever do is limit my interests and passions, and I wouldn't recommend that to anyone else. No matter what your OBT might be, you'll be better because you approach it from a wide variety of perspectives. I've always felt I was more creative because I love opera, magic, history, and theology. I bring those and other perspectives to the table to solve my creative problems.

> **There are more things in heaven**
> **and earth, Horatio, than are**
> **dreamt of in your philosophy.**
> —**William Shakespeare**, *Hamlet*, **act 1, scene 5**

I have a friend who has a unique corporate training program designed to help companies solve high-level challenges. If a company is struggling to design a new product, overcome an organizational hurdle, or break into a new market, they'll often send their top leaders to spend a few days at my friend's facility.

But what they encounter is not what they expect.

In one case a bicycle company came because they were stumped with a design flaw in a new concept bike. When they arrived, my friend had assembled a team—not of bike experts, but a military general, a heart surgeon, a college football coach, a novelist, and a housewife. Needless to say, the bicycle designers and executives were initially surprised and somewhat disappointed. But once they started discussing the problem, they were amazed by the different potential approaches. The surgeon looked at the flaw as an anatomical problem, the general as a battle strategy, the housewife as a family issue, and so on. Each brought unique questions, experiences, and ideas to the table.

By looking at the problem from these unique and unusual angles, they solved the design flaw on the project in record time. A flaw that had stumped bike experts for months was solved in a matter of days by bringing radically different thinking to the table.

In pursuit of your OBT, a wide variety of experience and expertise matters. Keep thinking, keep learning, and keep growing. Whatever you do, don't stop the guitar lessons, the dance classes, or the interest in astronomy. Keep reading and expanding your experience and perspective.

In the pursuit of life, a wide variety of activities can be challenging, stimulating, and inspiring. *But when it comes to your career, calling, or dream, understand that you won't get noticed for being pretty good at everything.* In today's cluttered and distracted world, in which your audience has an unlimited number of other choices, you'll only get noticed for being extraordinary at One Big Thing.

Malcolm Gladwell wrote a fascinating book a few years ago called *Outliers*, in which he studied the performance of a small group of people who fell outside statistical norms. In many cases, he applied what some call the 10,000-Hour Rule, which implies the top performers are dedicated, committed, and, because of extraordinary practice—at least 10,000 hours—excel beyond their competitors.

Obviously, many top performers seem *born* with extraordinary skill. When you compare their results with most of us, the athletic performance of Michael Jordan or Kobe Bryant, the investing success of Warren Buffett, the preaching ability of Billy Graham, or, before his passing, the visionary ideas of Steve Jobs are all outside the reference of most people. But the fact is, each of these people devoted many years of practice and study to his OBT.

> **When you can do the common things
> in an uncommon way, you'll command
> the attention of the world.**
>
> **—George Washington Carver, scientist,
> educator, and inventor**

Far too often, truly gifted employees and leaders have to fight the resistance of limited thinkers. As a result, not only do they have to excel in their fields, but have to carry the additional burden of closed-minded, insecure—and often underhanded—coworkers. But the phrase *a rising tide lifts all boats* is true. When a member of the team has exemplary gifts and talents, the best we can do is provide them with the resources they need, get out of the way, and enjoy their success.

One of the greatest reasons teams fail is because leaders don't know how to handle these high performers. Remember that individuals are not wellrounded. Each of us has strengths and weaknesses, and the best teams are groups where each of us complements each other. That's exactly why *teams* are well rounded, because individual people are not.

Getting the chemistry, the talent, and the vision of those individuals right is the most important task a team leader can accomplish. Recognizing the often incredible talent of high performers, or outliers, is a key part of that task.

In the case of outliers, you'll sometimes have a gifted person who can indeed do many things very well. But even in these rare cases, these remarkably talented individuals aren't known for their wide variety of talents, they're remembered for One Big Thing.

Some athletes like Michael Jordan are good enough to play multiple sports—even at the professional level. But although he can run circles around you and me in most sports, the truth is Michael will never be remembered for his uncanny skill on the baseball diamond.

He'll be remembered as a basketball legend.

WE LIVE IN A CLUTTERED WORLD

In 2008, I wrote a book called *Branding Faith: Why Some Churches and Non-Profits Impact the Culture and Others Don't*. It was one of the first books to bring the concept of branding into the nonprofit (and especially the religious) world.

But there were plenty of other branding books out there, so what made it different? I focused on the power of branding to distinguish your organization in today's cluttered, hypercompetitive world. How does your story cut through the clutter and actually get noticed? That's the key.

In 2011, I followed up with *Jolt! Get the Jump on a World That's Constantly Changing*, which was designed more for individuals. *Jolt!* was written to help people make their dream happen within a culture of overwhelming and disruptive change. Once again, I wrote the book in the context of the distracted, ADD culture we live in today.

Over the years, my work has been focused on *influence*. Helping people get noticed so their ideas can influence their family, their business, their customers, donors, and even the culture. From business leaders, politicians, community organizers, activists, pastors and religious leaders, nonprofit leaders, teachers, moms and dads—anyone who needs to influence another group, I'm interested in helping them make that happen.

But getting noticed in today's distracted world is a far greater challenge than any time in history. It seems like everyone is creating content and we're being flooded with new information. Video monitors have invaded gas pumps and elevators. Airports feature wall-sized TV screens spewing advertising information twenty-four hours a day. Billboards that used to be static have now become video screens so more information can be rotated regularly. Advertising agencies are finding more and more places to insert messages, from the trays we put our personal items into at airport security lines to the wall space in front of urinals.

Today technology is allowing companies to target us far more effectively—often without our even realizing it's happened. The movie *Minority Report* is coming true as advertisers are experimenting with billboards and other advertising that can actually recognize your features and display a promo customized for your sex and size—and one day, customized for *you*.

In fact, some researchers indicate we're being exposed to the phenomenal number of five thousand media messages per person, per day.[2] Distractions in the workplace have become so serious that *USA Today* reported that it costs a typical one thousand–employee company more than $10 million a year in lost productivity.[3]

The report goes on to indicate that more than half of US workers waste an hour or more a day from interruptions, and 60 percent come from electronic devices and e-mail. In fact, 45 percent of workers report that they can't go more than fifteen minutes without some sort of interruption. And it's no different during leisure time. Only 68 percent of people turn off their mobile phones during movies (which may explain the jerk three rows in front of you who keeps checking his e-mail). And at least half of all people leave on their mobile device when they go to bed.

In the NPR story, "Digital Overload: Your Brain on Gadgets," it was reported that the average person today consumes *three times* the information an average person consumed in 1960. They also cited a *New York Times* report that the average computer user checks websites forty times a day, and can switch programs thirty-six times an hour.[4]

As a result, that onslaught of messages, interruptions, and distractions is making it more and more difficult for any single message to connect with an audience.

Your movie idea now has to compete with multiscreen theaters, 3-D "event" movies, 500+ channel choices on cable or satellite TV, and literally millions of video downloads.

Your book now has to compete with thousands of self-published books from would-be authors, including your aunt Mabel's book on her life as a German immigrant.

Your brilliant idea for a nonprofit will have to compete for donor support with the more than 1.6 million nonprofit organizations that were registered with the IRS in 2011 alone.[5]

Your new business idea will have to compete for customers with the tens of thousands of new businesses opening each year (many of which fail soon after).

And don't get me started about the clutter that's descended on our lives with the advent of the Internet. According to Pingdom.com[6], here are a few standout numbers to give you an idea:

1.97 billion—*Internet users worldwide (as of June 2010).*
14%—*Increase in Internet users since the previous year.*
100 million—*New accounts added on Twitter in 2010.*
2 billion—*The number of videos watched per day on YouTube.*
3,000+—*Photos uploaded per minute to Flickr.*
3 billion+—*Photos uploaded per month to Facebook.*
20 million—*Videos uploaded to Facebook per month.*

We're swimming in media messages. There are lots of choices out there, and people are taking advantage of those choices. That's not to say it's impossible for you to get noticed, but today the equation of getting your message out there and finding an audience has dramatically changed.

» **A previous generation only needed a good idea and the motivation to sell it. Today the good idea still matters, but you also need to cut through all that clutter. The media jungle is thick, and, like Tarzan, you need a sharp blade.**

For instance:

Want to write a book?

With the advent of self-publishing, the number of books on the market is at an all-time high. According to R. R. Bowker, a leading source of publishing statistics,[7] more than 300,000 books were published last year in the United States, and nearly three million more were self-published. With self-publishing, you don't need a classic agent or traditional publisher to get your book on the market, which makes it easier than ever to actually turn your manuscript into a physical book. On the other hand, the flood of self-published books makes it tougher than at any point in history to get your book noticed by anyone other than your mom.

Even with the power and influence of traditional publishers, it's difficult enough to get coveted space on major bookstore shelves, and with self-publishing, it's almost impossible. I joke (halfway) that my previous book *Jolt!* was released in the same month that the Border's bookstore chain declared bankruptcy. (At least it supported the book's thesis that the world is changing faster than at any time in history.) But that made it even more competitive for us to find space on other retailers' shelves.

On average, a bookstore browser spends eight seconds looking at a book's front cover and fifteen seconds looking at the back cover. So with thousands of choices screaming out from the shelf, it's a real challenge to connect with an actual customer.

However, the numbers aren't impossible. According to the Author's Guild (authorsguild.org), a successful fiction book sells five thousand copies, and a successful nonfiction book sells seventy-five hundred copies. That means that if you have a built-in audience you can reach, the chances are much better. Pastors with a congregation,

CEOs with employees, customers, and vendors, or politicians with a constituency. Even social media followers represent potential audiences that might be interested in your book.

But make no mistake, yours is only one of the thousands of messages your audience deals with on a daily basis.

Want to launch a new company?

According to the US Department of Commerce, Bureau of the Census, Business Dynamics Statistics (how's that for a government name?), about a third of new firms only last two years, and only half survive five years. During the recent financial challenges worldwide, businesses were closing at record rates, and commercial real estate in most markets experienced great stress as more and more small businesses closed down.

At the same time, investment money was harder to find because the rich guys got hurt as well, and from the banking crisis to the mortgage mess—at least for the time being—people seem less likely to help launch a new business than in the past.

According to Robert Kelsey, author of *What's Stopping You?*, about half the population would like to run their own business, but only 5 percent actually do anything about it. Kelsey's reason? Fear of failure.

Want to make a movie?

Hollywood is tougher than ever, as the major studios focus on tent-pole films (big-budget blockbusters like *Pirates of the Caribbean*) or ultralow-budget entries that they support with very little marketing and promotion. Today, major producers, directors, and stars with incredible credits are out of work and struggling to make their mortgage payments.

At the same time, filmmakers haven't quite figured out the possibilities of online distribution. While Blockbuster declared bankruptcy, Netflix moved ahead, but with a major pricing snafu in 2011, the competition is seizing the moment. At the time I'm writing this chapter, Hulu—once thought to be the online savior of network TV—is struggling and being positioned for a sale.

Alternative distribution has always been a fascination for filmmakers. From distributing movies through social media platforms, church sanctuaries, or schools, any potential way to reach an audience is being explored.

But the sheer number of alternatives may be its undoing. As the alternatives increase, the clutter increases, making it even more difficult to find an audience large enough to support your work. It's fantastic that a hundred thousand people saw your ten-minute short film on YouTube, but that doesn't directly help you pay for the next project.

The shift in the magazine industry is a great illustration of the same point. When I was a kid there were only a handful of major, national magazines on the market. But today, there are literally thousands of niche magazines catering to ever smaller, more specialized audiences. According to the *Huffington Post*,[8] there are actual magazines called:

Meat Goat Monthly News
Teddy Bear Times
Mules and More
I Love Cats
Wood

You can pause your reading here if you'd like to race out and buy any of these magazines.

Want to create a nonprofit or humanitarian organization?

The world needs help more than ever, but donor dollars are getting harder to find in a more competitive giving environment. *Giving USA 2011*, the annual report on philanthropy in the United States released by the Giving Institute and Indiana University's Center on Philanthropy, indicates that giving by Americans increased slightly in 2010; however charities still are facing a long, uphill climb back to prerecession levels of growth and income.

Local church leaders will tell you that fund-raising has been a difficult slog over the last few years. I toured a social service facility recently here in Los Angeles, and they observed that while the need is rising, the donor dollars are not.

Part of the challenge is that with the ubiquity of social media, everyone is starting a "cause" these days. After being moved by the Haiti earthquake or the tsunami in Japan, great numbers of people started Facebook pages to try to raise money. While it's encouraging to see the concern, some are half-baked and actually divert giving from more established and proven relief organizations like the Salvation Army or the Red Cross.

Either way, there are thousands of mom-and-pop nonprofits these days for a variety of pet projects—all fighting to get noticed. While these are noble efforts and I applaud their vision and concern, the clutter increases.

ALMOST IMPOSSIBLE, BUT NOT QUITE

The common theme to each of these scenarios is that it's tougher than ever to fight for investors, donors, publishers, banks, studios, customers, moviegoers, or your boss's attention. The sheer competition makes it almost impossible to achieve our goals today.

》 **No matter how life-changing your message, without an audience that message doesn't matter.**

But in spite of these disheartening facts and figures, the truth is people succeed everyday. An unknown writer breaks through to write a best seller, a new business beats the odds and succeeds, a student filmmaker creates an award-winning movie, or a previously off-the-radar nonprofit makes a remarkable impact in a place of incredible need.

As I write this, the supposedly final film of the Harry Potter series is opening, and the author of the best-selling series of books— J. K. Rowling—has a remarkable story. Nearly broke, she began writing her first Harry Potter book in a coffee shop to keep warm. Despite the odds, she managed to become one of the world's richest women. She's one of only five self-made female billionaires, and the first billion-dollar female author.

》 **Success happens in spite of bad statistics, a terrible economy, and horrendous odds.**

Certainly there are lots of reasons some people break through and this isn't the place to discuss them all. Timing, background, determination, press coverage, buzz, fickle audiences, momentum, daddy's money, extraordinary quality, need, and much more contribute to successful projects, and as you look across the marketplace, those elements are often easy to spot.

But so is one other thing: a person or organization who discovered how to cut through the clutter and get noticed.

> **Out of clutter, find simplicity. From discord, find harmony. In the middle of difficulty, lies opportunity.**
> —**Albert Einstein, theoretical physicist**

In the past, all we had to worry about was being good at our job. We could focus on being the best CEO, writer, salesperson, teacher, filmmaker, or banker. While expertise is still critical, today we need something more to fight our biggest adversary, clutter.

In the office, financial cutbacks and reorganization strategies are forcing many of us to work harder. Technology has become a major distraction as executives try to balance face-to-face leadership with the increasing demands of our mobile devices.

> **Attention is one of the most valuable modern resources. If we waste it on frivolous communication, we will have nothing left when we really need it.**
> —**John Freeman, author of *The Tyranny of E-mail***

According to John Freeman, author of *The Tyranny of E-mail*:

- *65 percent of North Americans spend more time with their computers than their spouses.*
- *In 2009, it's been estimated the average corporate worker spent more than 40 percent of his or her day sending or receiving some two hundred e-mail messages.*

One Big Thing

- *In a world home to six billion people, roughly six hundred million e-mails are sent every ten minutes.*
- *E-mail is changing the way we read and communicate.*
- *77 percent of workers report that e-mail downtime causes major stress at work, with 10 percent actually assaulting their computers.*
- *E-mail is addictive in the same way slot machines have been shown to be addictive.*
- *As a result, some psychologists are actually pushing to have Internet addiction broadly classified as a clinical disorder.*

It's not hard to see that competition for our boss's attention is getting tougher than ever. I regularly attend corporate meetings with various clients and notice that no one in the meeting is actually looking at each other. They're all looking underneath the table checking e-mail on their mobile devices.

Meaninglessness reigns supreme: We are no longer amusing ourselves to death, we are texting ourselves to death.
—Neal Gabler, author and social critic

Ever notice that when you meet a colleague for lunch, the first thing each of you do is set your mobile device on the table—*just in case?* I mean, you never know when an e-mail message that could change the world will appear, so you always have to be ready, right?

On that subject, let me add that the most valuable commodity of the twenty-first century will be *undivided attention.* Want to give a wonderful gift to your spouse, your coworkers, your family, or a friend? Give them your undivided attention. In a world of growing and unrelenting distractions, your personal attention may be the greatest gift of all.

YOUR GREAT IDEA DOESN'T MATTER

Lose the audience, and it really doesn't matter how great your story is.
—Ryan Mathews and Watts Wacker, authors
of *What's Your Story? Storytelling to Move
Markets, Audiences, People, and Brands*

In a cluttered and distracted world, it doesn't matter how great your idea is—because if no one's listening, you've failed.

It doesn't matter that you have a brilliant strategy to solve your company's problems, because no one has the time to look at it or hear your plan.

It doesn't matter that you're producing the next Hollywood blockbuster, because you can't get anyone in the industry to read the screenplay.

It doesn't matter that you've written a potential *New York Times* best seller, because you can't interest a publisher.

It doesn't matter that you have the next killer app if it just lingers in the app store with a billion competitors.

It doesn't matter if your idea can change the world if the world isn't paying attention.

So what's the answer? How do you break through? How do you *or your ideas* get noticed?

Working with nonprofit organizations is, in many ways, far more challenging than working with a for-profit business. Nonprofits are usually selling what the customer doesn't want. It's not about selling something sexy, trendy, or cool. It's about selling a *need*—or perhaps more important, *the solution to a need*. The goal is for a potential donor to support a great cause—to help alleviate suffering, hunger, or poverty.

The question is, *what's in it for the donor*? Everyone gives for a reason. It might be a good reason—they want to make a difference, feel good, or change the world—or a little more selfish reason— they want their name on a building, to secure a tax deduction, or get recognized in the local paper.

Marketing and donor development strategies for nonprofit and religious causes are extensive, but there's one thing I've discovered that it takes to get nonprofits noticed: brilliant execution. In other words, they do One Big Thing extraordinarily well.

> » **In today's hypercompetitive, distracted, cluttered, ADD culture, the best way to get noticed is to be incredible at *one thing*.**

It may be building water wells in Africa, rescuing young girls from sex trafficking, helping the homeless, or pregnancy counseling. It might be a million different organizations doing a million different things—but each one gets on the radar of the public by being extraordinary at one thing.

After thirty years helping these wonderful organizations accomplish their missions, I've found that the most effective and successful way to cut through the clutter of competition from other causes is to simply be remarkable at One Big Thing.

In a distracted, hypercompetitive world, you can't just be decent at a number of different tasks. Too many people are pretty good, and that doesn't get you on the radar.

» **People don't pay for okay—they pay for *great*.**

It's important to keep in mind that once you're successful—once you've made it to the top—you can do anything you want. The Salvation Army, for instance, is a global organization that features programs and outreaches to the homeless, disaster relief, human trafficking, poverty, the elderly, those struggling with pornography, youth camps, and much more. It reaches into every corner of need and is making a remarkable impact around the world.

But when William Booth began his ministerial career in 1852, he focused on one thing: reaching the outcasts. Thieves, prostitutes, gamblers, and drunkards were among his first converts to Christianity. As the Salvation Army website says: "To congregations who were desperately poor, he preached hope and salvation. His aim was to lead people to Christ and link them to a church for further spiritual guidance."

William Booth started with one noble cause and was remarkable in his commitment.

For Don Stephens, it was building a floating hospital that become a global organization called Mercy Ships.

For Jackson Pollock, it was discovering how splatter could transform his art career.

For Steve Jobs, it was combining design elegance into a computer interface.

For Truett Cathy, it was creating the perfect chicken sandwich.

For Dean Koontz, it was writing thrillers.

For Jeff Bezos, it was selling books online.

For Guy Kawasaki, it was empowering people.

For Allison Krauss, it was bluegrass music.

Once they became successful, they could do anything they wanted. But to get noticed, they focused on One Big Thing.

What about you? What is the One Big Thing you were born to accomplish?

The journey begins . . .

Chapter Four

THE POWER OF ONE BIG THING

The Key to Having Influence

*In our pop cultural world, getting noticed
is by far the most difficult feat.*

—Christopher B. Hays, "The Folly of Answering Fools,"
Christianity Today

*We don't have to be a TV producer or serial-drama writer
to exert influence. We merely need to be good storytellers.*

—from *Influencer: The Power to Change Anything* (Patterson,
Grenny, Maxfield, and McMillan)

For me, it's ultimately about influence. Most of us would like to be rich and maybe even take a shot at being famous, but in the end, the most important thing you can possibly accomplish with your life is a legacy of influence.

Many people have a motivation to be influential, and in some cases, influence isn't only big, it's highly rewarded. Hollywood's *Variety* magazine reported in 2010 that Peter Chernin, chairman of the Chernin Entertainment Group, has the kind of influence that entertainment companies are willing to pay big money for. *Variety* reported that when cable giant Comcast purchased a majority stake in NBC, they were willing to pay Chernin one hundred thousand dollars *per consult*.

Influence can be rewarding indeed.

But real influence doesn't have to be on such a large scale—either in terms of money or audience. Your desire to influence your children or grandchildren; your desire to impact your company, church, or volunteer organization; your ability to influence the next generation is all tied into knowing and understanding your single-minded purpose.

Why? Because discovering your one thing will make you passionate, and people respond to passion. Passion is one of the most contagious emotions on the planet, and people will line up to follow it, especially when the passionate person has credibility.

In other words, if my neighbor gets passionate about exploring space I wouldn't get very excited because he's retired, overweight, and his chances of qualifying for the space program are zero. But should I meet a passionate young Air Force Academy graduate who's been accepted into NASA, then I want to hear what he has to say.

I can never say enough about the importance of credibility when it comes to influence. I once had an employee who had something to say about everything. Even during his first week as an intern, with no knowledge of television or media, he would chime into client meetings and offer his opinion about our strategies, ideas, and plans. While I'm always eager to hear new ideas, his input was completely irrelevant because he had no history or expertise in the field. Although I spoke to him privately about it, he just wouldn't shut up. His *passion* for media got way out ahead of his *expertise* in media.

As a result, everyone else around the table just ignored him.

>> **Brilliant ideas without a credible spokesperson are tough to sell.**

But those who are in pursuit of their One Big Thing are as attractive to people as paper clips to a magnet. People follow visionaries—especially those who know what in the world they're talking about.

> **Leaders have followers. Managers have employees. Managers make widgets. Leaders make change.**
> **—Seth Godin, marketing expert**

Influence isn't about giving orders. Anyone can do that. Far too many managers today think that a job title makes them a leader. Calling myself one doesn't make me a leader any more than calling myself a Corvette makes me a car. Backstage, at a business event where I had the opportunity to speak onstage with leadership expert John Maxwell, he told the audience, "If you think you're a leader, but no one's following you, then you're just out for a walk."

There's a very big difference between *ordering people around* and *leading change*. Movements happen because of the vision and passion of people with the credibility to inspire loyalty. Plenty of people *talked* about civil rights in the sixties, but only a handful of African American leaders could persuasively express their vision and strategy, plus endure arrest and jail. That powerful combination gave them enormous credibility over the hundreds of others who were simply shouting.

» Whom do you want to influence?

Whom do you want to influence? Start thinking about the answer to that question now because it will help you focus on your OBT. Perhaps more important, it will help you decide the knowledge and experience you need. In the book *Influencer: The Power to Change Anything*, the authors note, "Many of the profound and persistent problems we face stem more from a lack of skill (which in turn stems from a lack of deliberate practice) than from a genetic curse, a lack of courage, or a character flaw."

In other words, people's inability to change doesn't come from personal weakness, lack of boldness, or some type of shortcoming. In the vast majority of cases research proves again and again that people simply lack information—clearly defined skills. And I'm not just talking about a bad habit or weakness. Far too many people believe that they can't realize their One Big Thing because they can't marshal the discipline, focus, or ability to make it happen. But that's simply not true. During all these years that you thought your lack of self-discipline was holding you back, you were just believing a myth.

You simply didn't have the right skill set to make that change happen.
Real influence starts with that statement.

**Think twice before you speak,
because your words and influence
will plant the seed of either success
or failure in the mind of another.**

—Napoleon Hill, author and
personal-success speaker

Influence often happens when you apply the right tools to a passionate goal. Either one alone is a challenge, but together you can change people, change your company, or change your community.

As you develop your OBT, the possibilities for making a significant impact will begin to open up. As you gain expertise and credibility in an area you're extraordinarily passionate about, you'll immediately begin to influence the people around you.

It's tough not to notice a raging fire.

Chapter Five

THE POWER OF PERCEPTION

Is Your One Big Thing About Having a Brand?

You're just anybody without your identity.

—GRENVILLE MAIN, MANAGING DIRECTOR OF DNA DESIGN

Much of our shared knowledge about ourselves and our culture comes to us through a commercial process of storytelling called branding.

—JAMES B. TWITCHELL, FROM HIS BOOK *BRANDED NATION*

In 2003, Peter Montoya and Tim Vandehey wrote a book called *The Brand Called You*. Its subtitle was clear: *The Ultimate Brand-Building and Business Development Handbook to Transform Anyone into an Indispensable Personal Brand.* It was one of the first books designed to help anyone understand the power of a personal brand.

While a personal brand isn't the same as what I consider your OBT, I believe it's worth understanding what a personal brand is and how it impacts your perception.

Brands are important because perception matters. The 1969 BBC documentary, *Royal Family,* has been noted by many as a turning point in changing the perception of the royal family and the British crown. It featured Queen Elizabeth and her extended family watching TV, relaxing at home, and generally doing the ordinary activities of daily living—the very things the rest of us "normal folk" do.

However much that personal, behind-the-scenes film might have endeared the royal family to millions of subjects across the empire, it also largely dispelled the romance and aura of what happens behind the royal curtains. From that point on, some historians and royal watchers felt that the shine started to wear off the crown, and the British general public never again had that same sense of mystery and respect.

> **If general perception changes from seeing the glass as "half-full" to seeing it as "half empty" there are major innovative opportunities.**
>
> **—Peter F. Drucker, writer and management consultant**

I'm passionately motivated by my religious and nonprofit clients because they're making a real difference in the world. Whether it's feeding hungry children, building water wells in Third World countries, providing medical care, or helping people struggle with deep questions of faith, there are few things in life more satisfying than seeing lives changed on a global scale. I'm actually writing this chapter on a flight back to the States from New Delhi, India, where my wife, Kathleen, and I have been teaching at a conference for young creative leaders and working with a major nonprofit in that nation.

Years ago, I realized how many nonprofits and religious organizations don't understand their One Big Thing. Perhaps they were founded to fill a specific need, but over the years that need has expanded or changed. More often than not, they simply got distracted, and years later discovered they had lost effectiveness because they had wandered from their original vision.

Sounds like us, doesn't it?

Throughout the intervening years, I began discovering connections between a brand and your OBT. After all, your *influence* begins with discovering what you were born to accomplish. As a result, your *one thing* can be expressed in many ways—the reason you exist, your purpose for living, your destiny, or even what's been described as "what you were born to do"—while your *brand* involves your perception surrounding that thing. In other words, what do people think of when they think of you? While many branding experts have many different definitions of a brand, in my book, *Branding Faith*, I defined it as "a compelling story that surrounds a product, person, or organization." From an organizational perspective, the Kellogg School of Management at Northwestern University defines a brand as "the practice of delivering a promise that reflects the mission, uniqueness and personality of an organization."

The primary focus of your brand message must be on how special you are, not how cheap you are. The goal must be to sell the distinctive quality of the brand.
—Kerry Light, brand strategist

Whatever the specific definition, a brand is a perception of how people view what you do and how well you do it. That's why major corporations do their best (and often spend millions) on influencing and protecting their brand. We all have a brand because we all have perceptions that surround us. My friend and marketing expert Brad Abare uses a simple phrase I've never forgotten: Everything communicates.

EVERYTHING COMMUNICATES

Brad understands that everything we do communicates a message and to neglect that understanding is to neglect opportunities of influence. So our OBT and how we execute it will communicate a message, and how that message is perceived by our boss, our spouse, our customers, investors, donors, the general public—whoever—will have a great impact on our ability to be successful.

That's why I think it's worth taking a look at some insights about your personal brand. In Montoya and Vandehey's book, they shared three critical insights:

First, visibility is just as important as ability.

In a media-driven culture, being seen is just as important as being good. It sometimes makes people angry—but it's true. Today there are many thousands of brilliant, gifted professionals who will never make an impact because people don't know who they are.

You see the concept most clearly in Hollywood, where actors of little ability and skill make millions of dollars simply by being in the right place at the right time. On the other hand, as a producer and director, I'm amazed at the incredible level of talent among unknown actors I see in casting sessions. Men and women with incredible gifts, but who will never be recognized or known.

Colleges and universities are filled with professors who are brilliant in their individual fields, but because they don't know how to share that expertise with the world, they have little or no influence beyond the school's front gate.

In business, the people you see interviewed on television or listen to on the radio aren't necessarily the most gifted, skilled, or respected leaders out there.

Is Dr. Phil the best psychologist in America?

Is Dr. Oz the best doctor?

Is Brian Williams from NBC News the best reporter?

Is Judge Judy the best court judge?

Probably not. But they have influence because they have visibility.

Does ability matter? No question. Education, skill, expertise, and personal growth are critical. When the door opens you'd better be ready to act and have the talent and education to back it up. But unless that door opens, all the talent in the world will do little outside of entertaining your family.

Getting the story of your OBT out there isn't necessarily the act of an egotistical maniac. We've all seen narcissists, but the truth

One Big Thing

is, getting on the radar of the public is the first step toward exercising the power of a compelling personal brand.

It's really a question of belief. Do you believe in your purpose and calling enough to step up to the plate and swing for the fence? Do you believe in your message enough that you'll do whatever it takes for an audience to hear?

I grew up thinking that great writers and artists were popular because people just recognized their remarkable abilities. That somehow they transformed themselves into brilliant, successful artists with no effort at all. It was only later when I realized just how hard great writers like Ernest Hemingway fought to get their work in front of the reading public. They agonized over reviews, argued with editors, and pleaded with publishers. Getting your story out there is an uphill battle—even for the most talented among us.

> **Tell a good story, and you create a success. Tell a great story, and you can create a movement.**
>
> —Ryan Matthews and Watts Wacker, authors of *What's Your Story? Storytelling to Move Markets, Audiences, People, and Brands*

Second, Montoya and Vandehey believe that you can't brand a lie.

Certainly we should act with integrity, and every expression of your personality—both professionally and personally—should be true and honorable. But when it comes to your OBT, I find a great number of leaders take a shortcut. You've seen it in advertising or promotions for so-called experts on marketing, real estate, or motivation. They advertise and promote themselves as "global thought leaders," but they can't really back it up. Perhaps in a smaller way, you've done that in the past. To win a new client or land a new business deal we're tempted to add areas of expertise we don't really have, or experience that's never actually happened. How many résumés are slightly exaggerated?

> ## The truth does not change according to our ability to stomach it.
> —Flannery O'Connor, novelist

In the entertainment business, I'm used to hearing people stretch the truth about their influence or experience in the industry. One of the most repeated exaggerations is for someone to casually say, "I've worked at Fox"—implying that they've been employed by Fox News, Twentieth Century Fox, or the Fox Television Network. But once they're grilled, you discovered that they *actually* worked at a local Fox affiliate station somewhere in the Midwest.

Perhaps not an outright lie, but not quite the same thing as what's implied. When the truth is revealed, one's positive perception takes a beating.

As I write this chapter, New York Congressional representative Anthony Weiner was added to the growing list of men and women who've been exposed (in this case literally) for not matching their professional lives to their personal behavior. Not only did he allegedly "sext" photos of various body parts to young women he connected with through social media, he then lied about it to the American public. After the truth was exposed, he finally came clean, but not before his credibility was irreparably damaged and his career most likely destroyed.

On the other hand, being truthful and responsible can actually add to your reputation—even during periods of desperate challenge.

One of the classic stories is the famous "Tylenol scare" of the fall of 1982, when McNeil Consumer Products, a subsidiary of Johnson & Johnson, was hit with a major crisis when seven people on Chicago's West Side died mysteriously. After a brief investigation, it was determined that each of the people had taken an Extra-Strength Tylenol capsule laced with cyanide. When the news of the incident caused a massive, nationwide panic, Johnson & Johnson was forced to act. Realizing that millions of dollars were at stake, they could have hesitated, fought the accusations, and held up the investigation. But they immediately pulled millions of dollars of Tylenol from the shelves in a bold move to restore the public's trust, and by acting quickly, they accomplished what's since become a lesson in positive public relations.

Today, the Tylenol brand is a trusted name because consumers link it with integrity and public trust. Most others with similar crises have never recovered.

It's not about covering up, deflecting, or denying. On the contrary, it's about being truthful and confronting the media in a way that permits the real story to be told, without letting denials, information scraps, inaccuracies, and falsehoods color the story. When it comes to your personal reputation, the stakes are remarkably high.

It's also not simply about moral or financial failure, it's about gifts, talents, and expertise. If your OBT results in your becoming an expert on drug treatment, you'd better be able to back it up. If you promote the fact that you're a great business leader, you'd better have the credentials to prove it. If you teach on financial success, you'd better be making money somewhere.

Getting noticed is critically important, but once that happens, we need to be reminded that there's no substitute for real experience and accomplishment. We see so many experts on television and it's easy to think it must be simple to do what they're doing. But we often forget the years or sometimes decades they spent in the trenches of education, work, and life experience, learning the principles that allow them to speak at an influential, national level.

> **Your vocation is when your deep gladness and the world's deep hunger meet.**
>
> **—Frederick Buechner, American writer and theologian**

Discovering your One Big Thing is critical, but not enough. You also need to do something with it. I've heard it said that we should find the intersection between our passion and the world's great need. But in stepping out boldly to activate our purpose, we have to remember integrity and honesty.

Remember—this is the age of social media. With a few easy keystrokes on a computer, anyone can be investigated, anytime. Politicians are finding this out in the heat of campaigns as old DUI convictions suddenly pop up, a racist remark is uncovered through the Internet, or embarrassing or forged academic records are revealed.

Today, we live in a world of video cameras, databases, and information retrieval. Controversies rage almost daily about mobile phones tracking our locations, Internet marketers recording our buying habits, and e-mails being exposed publicly.

❯❯ Never in history have leaders of all kinds needed to be more transparent.

In fact, Internet search engines aren't just about *search*, they're about *reputation management*. For a generation of young people who grew up posting the most intimate details of their lives on the Web, they're finding that in their twenties, it's getting tough to find a job. Once the interview is complete, the first thing a future employer often does is an online search, only to find the old drinking photos from the college dorm, a raging political rant, embarrassing personal details, explicit sexual stories, and more.

Hardly welcome news for a prospective employer.

In the old days, executives, politicians, and religious leaders could have a private jet, a luxury car, a mistress, or a mansion and few would ever find out. But today a few keystrokes on the computer reveal everything.

Brands are the express checkout for people living their lives at ever increasing speed.
—from *Brandweek* magazine

Third, in a media-driven culture, being different is everything.

This may be the closest connection between Montoya and Vandehey's ideas on personal branding and discovering your OBT. The world isn't looking for a copy of an existing writer, musician, politician, CEO, or leader; they're looking for someone new, innovative, and original. God gave you a unique DNA, so your job is to discover how your unique gifts and talents can differentiate you from everyone else.

You have no idea the number of people who call our offices each week asking us to "do the same thing for us that you did for your national clients." They want to copy someone they admire, and they're asking us to help get that story out there and get noticed by the national media. But they've got it backwards. There's already one of those famous leaders. A *new* person needs to emphasize his or her unique differences.

Besides, each of our clients were unique and brilliant long before I ever met them. Probably the most powerful gift these leaders had was an understanding of who they were and what their talent and calling were about.

That's something worth repeating: *Probably the most powerful gift these leaders had was an understanding of who they were and what their talent and calling were about.*

Having an accurate understanding of what makes you unique and different is absolutely critical. For many, an accurate understanding is obscured or undermined by a lack of professionalism, bad ideas, poor taste, inept leadership, insecurity, lack of people skills, bad assumptions, and more. These sorts of things plague many leaders today and hamper their effectiveness.

Listen to Apple Computer ads and "Think Different." If God created you as a completely unique individual, what does that mean for the type of vision you're called to accomplish?

Most of us live our entire lives as strangers to ourselves. We know more about others than we know about ourselves. Our true identity gets buried beneath the mistakes we've made, the insecurities we've acquired, and the lies we've believed.

—Mark Batterson, author of *Soul Print: Discovering Your Divine Destiny*

What makes you different from all the others competing for your position?

There's even more competition out there within the greater culture. In today's world, everybody competes.

For media creators, product producers, sales professionals, and more—how can you compete with all the entertainment choices, lifestyle options, or new digital technologies that struggle for the limited time of the average person today? You may not have the resources, finances, or assets the competition has, but you can tell a better story, and the key to finding that story is discovering what makes you unique and different.

What could it be that makes you different? Perhaps it's your unique communications style, your writing ability, your personality, or an expertise in an unusual area. Being different can mean many things, including perspective, content, skill, and delivery.

If competition from others is making it more difficult to get noticed, then perhaps you should consider a different niche. Some organizations have decided that because of duplication of services by other companies in the area, they should find a different way of doing their work or do it in a different place.

Hollywood is particularly good at this; studios track what other studios are developing so they don't release a similar film. Corporations spend enormous amounts of money following their competition's product development.

Even smart employees watch for potential changes in company staffing or structure to ensure they don't get pushed out of a job because of duplication or competition. It's not about conniving or cheating behind the scenes—it's about being aware and sensitive to the future.

Ultimately, it's all about authenticity. Being unique and different shouldn't mean *fake*. In our efforts to relate to the culture or a potential customer or audience, we sometimes go over the top and end up conveying a message that's obviously dishonest and far from authentic.

I'm told I was born with the gift of saying what everyone else in the room is thinking. Whether it gets me in trouble or not, I often feel compelled to talk about the elephant in the room that everyone else sees but ignores. That's why this issue of authenticity is so important for me. I was born with a very sensitive BS button, and anytime a client presents an advertisement, website, TV program, or other presentation that smacks of insincerity, I light up.

> **» Too many people think that developing or influencing their own brand is about becoming something they aren't, when it's really about discovering what they truly are.**

I regularly meet people who live out others' dreams and refuse to act on who they were created to be. What about you? Have you watched your boss so closely that you've started becoming more like him or her than you? Have you followed a celebrity to the point where his or her style is obscuring your own? Have you followed trends to the point it's difficult to discover what's really inside you? Don't become something you aren't; developing a personal brand is about becoming who you truly are.

It happens even in the best of ways. One friend got involved in raising money to build medical facilities in Third World countries. It was a great cause and she certainly could have spent her life doing worse. Ultimately, it wasn't really her passion. But she put off confronting that fact for years because it was such a great cause.

The problem was—it just wasn't *her* cause. When she finally had the courage to step out into something she was personally passionate about, she had already wasted years of productivity.

I know others who are trapped working in a company, church, or humanitarian organization who—although they do great work—are settling for second best in their lives. I can see they have so much more potential, but when I bring it up, they rationalize it with the importance of the cause, the need, or the great work they're doing. They've been sucked into a regular paycheck, or refuse to change because they're not willing to risk taking a hard look at their lives, their gifts, and their future.

I understand, because I've been there.

>> **Ultimately, a significant part of being different is being honest about who you are and how you're perceived.**

Finding your honest voice in the middle of the madness is absolutely critical. But being absolutely truthful about what distinguishes you from the pack is a critical step to finding your identity. I believe God made everyone unique and different, and that's why finding that distinctive combination is the key to understanding your One Big Thing.

Chapter Six

THE POWER OF VALUES

*Why Your One Big Thing Must Express
Who You Really Are*

Personal leadership is the process of keeping your vision and values before you and aligning your life to be congruent with them.

—STEPHEN COVEY, LEADERSHIP CONSULTANT AND WRITER

You have brains in your head. You have feet in your shoes.
You can steer yourself in any direction you choose.

—FROM *OH, THE PLACES YOU'LL GO,* BY DR. SEUSS

One of the most competitive categories of computer apps these days is the category everyone terms *productivity*. Mostly filled with to-do and task manager programs, they are driven largely by the popularity of David Allen's book *Getting Things Done*. Getting your to-do list out of your head and down on a page is incredibly important, but rather than the old days of simply using a legal pad, there are now apps that help you define priorities, schedule tasks, put them in categories, assign tags, and more.

I'm a big fan of productivity apps because I've discovered that half the battle of getting things *done* is just getting them *down*. Grabbing a swirling list of things to do out of my head and ordering them in a prioritized list helps me relax. At least I'm not as worried that I'm forgetting something.

But the greatest aspect of these apps for me is priorities— highlighting the tasks on the list that really matter. Imagine making daily decisions without a sense of what's important. Do I work on my new books, or answer e-mails? Do I plan my wife's birthday or work on a blog post? Do I do my taxes or fix the plumbing problem?

Every day is made up of many decisions based on what's really important. In fact, I would go so far as to say that most unsuccessful people are unsuccessful because they either can't or won't decide on the important priorities in their lives.

PRIORITIES ARE DRIVEN BY VALUES

The secret to understanding your priorities is values. Values are the bumpers on the bowling alley of life. They determine our boundaries—how far we'll go on questionable issues. Knowing what matters—what you value—is absolutely key to living a life of meaning and purpose, and your values are critical steps to identifying your one thing. Why? Because your OBT will never contradict your values.

Will I compromise my marriage by clicking on that pornographic website?

Is it really worth stretching the truth on that client report at work in order to expand my business?

When the boss asks, is it okay to lie about a coworker I'm competing with for a promotion?

Can I fudge a little on my tax form?

Will anyone really notice if I change a few numbers on my expense report?

I'm on a business trip and my wife will never know about this one fling with a stranger . . .

> **Until you value yourself, you won't value your time. Until you value your time, you will not do anything with it.**
> **—M. Scott Peck, psychiatrist and best-selling author**

Values determine what's important and help determine your daily decisions. And while values influence the big choices—your chances of cheating on your spouse, robbing a bank, or killing your neighbor—they also govern a million small decisions we make every day.

Far too many people don't take their values seriously when it comes to the smaller things in life. But in many ways, that's the most important arena of all. After all, what are the chances that most of us will rob a bank or kill a coworker?

Don't answer that.

But what about damaging the reputation of a coworker we're competing with for a raise? How many times have we criticized him or her in an e-mail or privately to the boss? How many times have we left him or her holding the bag on a big project when we could have easily stepped in to help?

And what about money? Have you ever fudged the truth on your taxes? Or added a little in your expense reimbursement? Or "adjusted" the truth explaining to your wife why you were late?

Every day we have multiple opportunities to express our values and, frankly, many of us drop the ball. But what seems like something insignificant now can easily become something huge tomorrow.

> ## We may define therapy as
> ## a search for value.
> **—Abraham Maslow, psychologist and philosopher**

The problem really isn't having values; the problem is living them out. Sure we all value honesty, integrity, and forgiveness, but when pressed, do we really live them out? And what about when it costs us? Are we willing to be honest when it's so easy to change our tax return? Or tell the truth when it comes to helping a coworker get the raise you want? Supporting your husband when he's driving you crazy or not paying attention to you?

Pursuing a life of value can be costly. It comes with a price. But what we exchange for that price is the ability to hold our head high during the day and sleep well at night. Perhaps just as important, it allows us to relax. The mental toll of cheating, lying, or stealing is draining. Trying to remember the lie you told your boss the last time, so today's lie will match up can literally wear you out. You'll never maximize your One Big Thing without living within the framework of your values.

Over the years I've had the opportunity to work with a few TV and movie producers who I discovered were unscrupulous in their pursuit of a profit. They would undercut vendors, damage relationships, and disregard agreements. I have no idea how they look at themselves in the mirror or sleep at night. One thing I can say with great satisfaction is that in each case they are either out of the business or created such a bad reputation that few will work with them anymore.

» Compromising your values catches up with you.

The truth is, we all face the temptation to disregard our values from time to time, and it usually happens because of pressure. Pressure from peers, those in authority, or time. In these cases, locking in your values is something you absolutely must do now before you're placed in the heat of battle.

For instance, I've been in conference meetings in which the CEO quietly suggested we stretch the truth in an advertising campaign. While some might convincingly say that all advertisements stretch the truth a bit, in this situation he was asking us to outright lie. There was enormous pressure. Here we were with the corporate leadership team, millions of dollars on the line, and a deadline approaching.

I knew walking away would cost me the account, but I did it anyway. It simply wasn't worth risking a reputation that had taken years to build.

Values count in Hollywood too. When a director approaches you on the set to push your sexual boundaries in a scene, I counsel young actors that's not the time to decide what those boundaries are. With up to sixty crew members standing around waiting, a lot of money hanging in the balance, your career before you, and the clock ticking, you simply aren't in a frame of mind to make a good decision.

It's far better to have settled it earlier, without the social and time pressure of the moment.

> ## Education without values, as useful as it is, seems rather to make man a more clever devil.
> —C. S. Lewis, author of *The Chronicles of Narnia*

Values matter. They're the map on the journey of self-discovery that leads to your OBT. Discovering your purpose without a sense of values is like being unable to make a decision about which turn to make. In many ways our culture has lost its sense of values; I worry about a generation that's been brought up afraid to make choices for fear of offending someone.

Multiculturalism teaches us that all cultures should be valued at the same level. Society teaches us that there's no such thing as evil, it all depends on your environment. School leaders try to tell us that boys and girls are the same, when any parent knows better. We've become a culture afraid to make judgments and proscribe values to anything because of our overwhelming fear of offending.

But something inside knows that's not true. Some choices are better than others. Some decisions make sense and others don't.

Values matter.

The truth is, values help keep us on the right road in pursuit of our OBT. And when we discover our purpose, values are what help us make the right decisions regarding it.

No amount of ability is of the slightest avail without honor.

—Andrew Carnegie, industrialist, businessman, and philanthropist

Your power to choose is remarkable. Your ability to change your life is directly connected to your ability to make choices and to take responsibility for those choices.

In other words, your daily decisions determine your destiny.

The point is that your One Big Thing needs to be aligned with your values. Whatever you choose to do with your life can't contradict or conflict with your basic values.

One of the most important questions to ask is, *Where do my values come from?* For me, the answer would be that they come from the Judeo-Christian tradition and are based on the Bible. Reverence for God, the value of life, the importance of marriage and family, the loyalty to truth, humility—all of these values come from that tradition. Do people keep them perfectly? Sadly, no. But if your life is based on these values, then your goal should be to make them real in every project, idea, or assignment you pursue.

Others use different value systems based on different foundations. How about you? Without values, you'll never make strong decisions, because you'll never have a solid base. The foundation of your life is what gives you the confidence to make decisions, and the critical importance of values is the key.

Once you have a sense of the things that matter, then you're in a position to close in on your One Big Thing.

Chapter Seven

WHAT'S YOUR ONE BIG THING?

The Question Only You Can Answer

*Most people think they know what they're
good at. They are usually wrong.*

—Peter F. Drucker, writer and business consultant

A great man is one sentence.

—Clare Booth Luce, socialite, ambassador,
  and US Congresswoman

The 2007 film, *Freedom Writers*, starring Hilary Swank, was based on the book, *The Freedom Writers Diary*, by Erin Gruwell, a teacher at Woodrow Wilson Classical High School in Long Beach, California. The movie title is actually a play on words, referencing Freedom Riders, the multiracial civil rights activists who in 1961 pushed the limits of Supreme Court decisions regarding the desegregation of interstate bus travel.

The story in the film takes place in 1994 and focuses on Gruwell, who leaves her upscale hometown in Newport Beach to teach at a recently integrated inner city high school. She discovers she's been placed in a class of at-risk high school students—not the higher achieving students she was expecting. But after enormous struggle with the challenge of outside influences on their lives, she slowly begins to earn their trust by teaching them how to write the story of their lives.

Actress Hillary Swank and a powerfully compelling script do a brilliant job of showing how Erin Gruwell discovered her One Big Thing—helping her students share the story of their lives on paper. Initially Gruwell was idealistic, but ideals don't take you very far when the going gets tough. As she began really connecting with these students and understanding the backgrounds, family difficulties, and obstacles they had to overcome, her idealism gave way to a real burden, which changed everything.

Some people seem to be born with a real passion in life—to excel in sports, become an activist, change the world, share their faith, write, and more. I've always thought they were lucky. They have a pretty well-defined vision for their lives; some even seem "called" as children. I've had a number of people tell me they don't have that passion. Many struggle to find it. They are sincere people, and many have spent years looking for their purpose.

Why are you here? Why were you born? What dream keeps you up late at night?

WHAT ABOUT PERSONALITY TESTS?

Discovering your one thing isn't about formulas, intelligence tests, or questionnaires. But the more you understand about your personality, your wiring, your strengths and weaknesses, the better. It wasn't until midpoint in my career that I took personality tests seriously. A friend introduced me to the DiSC Profile and it literally changed the way I looked at my life. I'm not an advocate of any particular test or profile, but DiSC is the one I'm most familiar with.

The DiSC Profile is a series of questions that classify four aspects of behavior by testing word associations. By analyzing these word associations, it creates a quadrant that indicates stronger or weaker aspects of your personality.

DiSC is an acronym for:

- **D**ominance—*focusing on control, power, and assertiveness*
- **I**nfluence—*relating to social situations and communication*
- **S**teadiness—*relating to patience, persistence, and thoughtfulness*
- **C**onscientiousness—*relating to structure and organization*

For instance (and in simplistic terms), scoring high on the D scale might indicate your strength in leadership. Too far, however, might indicate a domineering personality that works against you as a leader. High I indicates what we might call a "people person"— someone who enjoys relating to people, is a strong communicator, and potentially has great influence. High S might indicate you're a loyal worker or team player, while a high C might point out your organizational ability or attention to detail.

In my case, I'm an off the chart I person. I love being around people, working with teams, and leading great projects. I've always known that, but after taking the DiSC profile, it was confirmed in black and white. For the first time, I was able to understand my wiring and realized my strengths and weaknesses weren't something to be ashamed of, but celebrated.

On the negative side, the test clearly confirmed that I'm not a detail person, and I'm certainly not the loyal, steady guy slaving away for years, unnoticed in cubicle number forty-seven. But tragically, for years I struggled with that guilt, endlessly searching for a technique, a software program, the right notebook—*something* that would help me deal with the disorganized details of my life.

I hated balancing a checkbook, and just the sight of an IRS tax form sent me into catatonic shock. You should see my personal filing cabinet.

Pitiful.

STOP WORRYING SO MUCH ABOUT YOUR WEAKNESSES

But taking the DiSC profile made me realize these aspects were deeply ingrained in my personality—not something I will ever be able to change. So I began looking for ways to focus more on my strengths and less on my weaknesses.

I first encountered the concept of spending less time working on our weaknesses from leadership expert John Maxwell. In my case, at one point I was so frustrated with my inability to balance a checkbook that I focused on it for six months. I thought, I'm a middle-aged man and should *at least* be able to balance my own checkbook.

And after six months I was doing much better—until I realized that on a scale of 1 to 10 if I was a 1 or 2 at the start, after six months of practice I was still only a 4 or 5 at best. It dawned on me that when it comes to skill, people don't pay for 4 or 5, they pay for 9 and 10. So I dropped the checkbook, turned it over to a bookkeeper, and started focusing on my strengths.

The DiSC profile liberated me to enjoy my strengths and stop worrying about my weaknesses. My only regret is that I didn't discover this miracle in my twenties. I wonder how much more productive and successful I'd be had I had a twenty year head start on feeling that freedom to pursue areas where I was the most confident.

EXPLORE YOUR PERSONALITY

Another classic profile is the Myers-Briggs Type Indicator. It focuses on how people make decisions and perceive the world. I know many who are devoted to Myers-Briggs, and it's another great tool. The assessment determines sixteen types, which are referred to by an abbreviation of four letters—the initial letters of each of their four type preferences (although it's a bit different for *intuition*, which uses the abbreviation N to distinguish it from *introversion*).

For instance:

ESTJ: *extroversion (E), sensing (S), thinking (T), judgment (J)*
INFP: *introversion (I), intuition (N), feeling (F), perception (P)*

And the designations continue for all sixteen personality types. For more information, you should check The Myers and Briggs Foundation at www.myersbriggs.org.

There are other popular (and simpler) methods. Tom Rath's Strengths Finder series, for example, includes the book, *Strengths Finder 2.0*, in which Rath gives the reader a computer code to access a questionnaire on a website. Marcus Buckingham's *Go Put Your Strengths to Work* is another excellent book on the subject, and allows you to tap into a website, short films, and other helpful resources.

Both writers help you understand that we spend far too much time trying to overcome our weaknesses, and not nearly enough time enhancing our strengths. Public speaking is a wonderful skill, but if it's not a strength, stop agonizing over your inability and start focusing on where you can thrive.

IS KNOWING YOUR PERSONALITY ENOUGH?

I can't say enough about exploring personality profiles. It's fascinating insight that, in my case, relieved me from a lot of guilt and helped release my strengths toward my life's purpose.

But is that enough?

Throughout my lifetime I've seen the trends toward different ways of understanding your purpose. In the fifties and sixties the focus was about a *role* and the point was to place people in the right *position*. In those days there were tests to determine whether you'd be a good manager, salesperson, or teacher. My mom was a college graduate, but shortly after graduation took a personality test that told her she'd be a good secretary. Regardless of potential or passion for anything else, she dutifully answered an ad for a secretarial job at a local used car lot, and stayed there for a number of years.

Now the trend is toward personality—or as some might call it, wiring. The goal is to get to the heart of your personality traits to discover key areas such as thinking, judgment, intuition, dominance, introversion, or extroversion.

Knowing as much as possible about your strengths and your personality type is critical, but to answer the bigger question of your one thing, it's not quite enough.

Your OBT isn't about a role—although it will certainly influence the job, project, or mission to which you dedicate your life. It's also not about personality—although your personality will have a huge impact on the choices you make.

FINDING THE RIGHT SEAT ON THE BUS

In 2001, Jim Collins published the now classic book *Good to Great: Why Some Companies Make the Leap . . . and Others Don't*. One of Collins' great concepts is his analogy of an organization being like a bus. Essentially, the CEO is the bus driver and provides the vision for where the bus needs to go. But he also has to get the right people on the bus, the wrong people off the bus, and then get the right people into the right seats.

It's a brilliant illustration. And the element of that analogy that strikes at the heart of the One Big Thing concept is finding the right seat on the bus. I believe millions of people work their entire lives without finding their place in the world. They work at the wrong job, dream the wrong dream, and pursue the wrong goals because they don't have an accurate assessment of their own personality.

They mean well and have the best motives, but believe a lie. They don't really understand how they're wired or how to use that knowledge to their advantage. As a result, they live a life of frustration—continually hitting the lid of their own limitations. I spent years thinking I was capable of roles totally outside my zone, and it wasn't until I realized my real strengths and weaknesses that I was free to let go of the things that were frustrating me and holding me back.

» **Having an accurate understanding of your own personality and wiring can help you understand your place in the company or on the team and help enhance your interactions with people. That alone could transform your life.**

There's a software company in Silicon Valley led by a good man we'll call Robert. Robert is experienced in the tech world and has enormous knowledge about how start-ups are run and operated. He's a hard worker and, after founding the company, named himself CEO.

The problem is he's not a CEO.

Generally speaking, in the world of creative companies the best leaders are charismatic and outgoing. They are engaging and inspiring, not to mention wildly innovative. But Robert, on the other hand, is exactly the opposite. He's methodical, organized, and more interested in minutia than vision. When clients or investors come to the office for meetings and have lunch brought in, the other members of his company bring the clients into the kitchen, enjoy the food, interact socially, and enjoy their time together. But

Robert quietly comes out of this office, fills his plate with food, turns, and shuffles back into his office and shuts the door.

In the tech world, certainly, investors want to fund a company because of brilliant, creative work. But they also want a company led by someone with vision—someone who's engaging, someone they enjoy being with.

But from a personality point of view, Robert rarely connects with potential clients, customers, or investors. As a result, his company has never made a real profit, has amassed a significant amount of debt, and is continually cutting back on employees as business dries up. Because he provided no vision, the handful of employees who have stayed just count their days, and in some cases have stolen money from the company. No matter how many creative ideas the company develops, people just don't enjoy the culture Robert has created.

Robert is not incompetent, and he's not a bad guy. In fact, he's a wonderful family man. He's just in the wrong seat on the bus. He desperately wants to be CEO, and because he founded the company, he can be whatever he wants. But because he's more of a COO or a manager, he doesn't see that his personality is limiting his effectiveness.

It's important to note it's not just about talents, gifts, ability, or intention. Robert has an encyclopedic knowledge of the software industry and the best of intentions. But Robert's personality doesn't fit the role he's taken at the company. As a result, it's damaged their business and alienated very talented employees who grew frustrated not seeing the organization fulfill its potential.

What Robert refuses to realize is that if he stepped back and allowed a truly gifted and visionary leader to take that particular seat on the bus, his company would grow and his income would potentially skyrocket. Robert could then refocus on his gift of *operations*, not *leadership*.

Getting the right people in the right seats on the bus could be the issue that's keeping your company from reaching the next level too. Perhaps more important, it could be the issue that's keeping *you* from reaching the next level.

How many Roberts do you know? Men and women who aren't bad or unqualified—just in the wrong place.

> **You never find yourself until
> you face the truth.**
> —Pearl Bailey, from her 1968
> autobiography *The Raw Pearl*

A personality test or evaluation isn't a magic bullet that will immediately solve all your problems, but there is one thing that will transform your life:

THE IMPORTANCE OF BRUTAL HONESTY

George Lang was born in Hungary in 1924 and eventually emigrated to the United States. His only real possession was hope, and his great dream was to be a violinist—or so he thought. After escaping a labor camp and probable execution during World War II, Lang fled to New York in 1946 with little money, even less English, and only his dream of becoming a concert violinist. He practiced and practiced, always holding onto the vision. But after hearing a remarkable violin concert by famed performer Jascha Heifetz, he realized his future pointed in a different direction.[10]

Interviewed on television many years later, he remarked that the concert was a moment of revelation. He realized that he could never be "a Heifetz with the violin," so he'd become "the Heifetz of something else."[11] He turned to the restaurant business and worked his way up the ladder to eventually owning the highly acclaimed Café des Artistes in New York City. Having built an international reputation, he even became a highly respected food critic and correspondent for CBS News.

» In what field could you become a Heifetz?

I loved Lang's brutal honesty in that interview. His realization that he would most likely never achieve his original dream didn't cause him to give up, grow bitter, or live in a delusion. He had the courage to face his limitations with brutal honesty and his clarity of vision enabled him to become just as influential in another area.

Perhaps even more, no matter how much he loved playing, he wasn't interested in becoming an average violin player—or an average anything else. He was only interested in finding the niche where he could be the best.

Until you start looking at your past, your present, and your future in brutally honest terms, you'll never be able to make the decisions that can transform your life. One thing that takes companies from "good to great" is their ability to look at all aspects of their performance in the cold, hard light of day. They create accountability and mechanisms for feedback so they know immediately if they're on the wrong track.

You don't have to be a big company—you can build mechanisms in your own personal life to give you accurate indicators to keep you on track as well. Are you listening to your customers and employees? Are you open to suggestions and advice? Are you aware of what the competition is doing? Are you up to date on the industry? Do you have an honest understanding of your own strengths and weaknesses? Would your coworkers, customers, and friends agree with that understanding?

> **It's better to hang out with people better than you. Pick out associates whose behavior is better than yours and you'll drift in that direction.**
> —Warren Buffett, investor and philanthropist

One important note: listening to feedback from people on your payroll is helpful, but has limitations. In most cases, you'll never get a brutally honest perspective on your performance from someone who depends on you for a paycheck. Business and nonprofit leaders are especially susceptible to this when they only listen to the advice and feedback from employees or their leadership team. In the best of all possible worlds it might work, but rarely in the real world. Don't delude yourself here. Make sure you have relationships with people who are knowledgeable *and* have nothing to lose by telling you the truth.

Chapter Eight

THE MAP OF YOUR FUTURE

Road Signs on the Journey to the One Big Thing

Wheresoever you go, go with all your heart.

—CONFUCIUS, CHINESE PHILOSOPHER

Every day you may make progress. Every step may be fruitful.
Yet there will stretch out before you an ever-lengthening,
ever-ascending, ever-improving path. You know you will
never get to the end of the journey. But this, so far from
discouraging, only adds to the joy and the glory of the climb.

—WINSTON CHURCHILL, FROM "PAINTING AS A PASTIME,"
PUBLISHED IN *THE STRAND MAGAZINE* (1921)

Your One Big Thing is really the quest for what you were put on the earth to accomplish, and it's the key to getting noticed—or getting your voice heard. It's not about a particular job or personality type, it's more about your purpose. Admittedly, it's difficult to pin down because it *could* lead to a particular job. However, I view your OBT as an overarching purpose that you could potentially fulfill in many different ways.

I produce television programs and films, write books, speak at conferences and events, write a blog, and consult with various clients—but my OBT is to help people and organizations engage their culture more effectively. Whatever it takes to make that happen, I'm ready to try.

Whatever it is for you, it's what makes you unique.

In the book, *Ignore Everybody*, writer and cartoonist Hugh MacLeod puts it this way: "A Picasso always looks like Picasso painted it. Hemingway always sounds like Hemingway. A Beethoven symphony always sounds like a Beethoven symphony. Part of being a master is learning how to sing in nobody else's voice but your own."

What's your voice?

For MacLeod, it was the moment he discovered drawing on the backs of business cards. But it's not just the form or the platform, ultimately it's the calling, the voice, the purpose.

> **Always remember that you are**
> **unique. Just like everybody else.**
> **—Despair.com**

Despite the joke at Despair.com, in a world of interchangeable people you need to stand out. Unions played a vital role earlier in the twentieth century, helping unite workers and speak as one voice to industrial corporations. Unions helped create safer coal mines, drive better regulations in the workplace, and create higher wages and benefits. But today unions are on the wane because the flipside of unionization is building interchangeable workers.

In today's economy there are millions of interchangeable workers, but what we need are people who stand out.

People who get noticed.

People who do remarkable things.

The question becomes, what's your unique voice? What's your purpose for living? What remarkable thing were you put on the earth to accomplish?

Only you can answer that question, but its answer is the key to your success. Whatever your dream—a book, movie, TV program, Web-based business, nonprofit organization, retail store, academic career, music, performance, whatever—discovering your one thing is the key to getting that dream noticed.

If you're not enjoying your work and you're not truly being who you can be, it's such a terrible waste of life. It's a huge part of who you are, not just in terms of time but in terms of energy and it dictates the big decisions you take in life such as where you live and who your friends are. If you're not really living through your work, then you're not really living.
—Chris Barez-Brown, British creativity coach

There's no foolproof formula or series of checkboxes for discovering your one thing, but if you ask the right questions, you can begin to open the curtain on the answer. From this moment, slow down, take your time, and start reflecting. While they may seem easy at first, each of these questions is critically important to your future:

QUESTION #1: WHAT COMES EASY TO YOU?

It may be a difference in individual style, but when it comes to *personal* organization, I think my wife, Kathleen, is a mess. She would disagree, of course, but her computer desktop is crammed with files, her desk is a veritable museum of knickknacks, paperweights, receipts, reminders, and more. She even has a large round antique table next to her desk that's filled with piles of paper. When I have the audacity to ask if she knows where something specific is, she barks at me that she knows the location of anything she needs—then tells me to leave the room so she can spend the next three hours searching for that lost receipt.

Typical creative person.

But when it comes to organizing something *big*—a conference, a wedding, a concert, or some other event—she's brilliant. She can schedule the process, lead a team, motivate volunteers, hit deadlines, and accomplish things that would put me in the loony bin.

She's known this all her life, and as a result, she's always received the call when something needs to be launched. When we got married, she was an elementary school teacher in Oklahoma. But it wasn't long before her organizational skills were exposed throughout the school district, and the local high school asked her to redesign the cheerleading and dance team program. She stepped in and within a year turned it into an award-winning powerhouse program.

Years later when our kids were in the Burbank High School show choir, we became copresidents of the booster club. I did the schmoozing and she did the organization. (I think we're a perfect team.) Once again, she helped manage a program with four choirs and hundreds of students, and helped create the foundation for Burbank High to become one of the premier show choirs in the nation. Eventually, the wildly successful TV program, *Glee*, was based partly on the Burbank choir program.

For a number of years, she codirected the Biola Media Conference—at the time, the largest conference in the country for people of faith working in Hollywood. Held at the CBS Studios lot every spring, it became a significant force for encouraging and motivating people to impact the culture through media and entertainment.

The bottom line is Kathleen has always been good at organizing people and events. While it's always a big job and certainly a lot of work, it is much easier for her than most other people because she is a natural. It is something that comes easy. *The irony is she spent many hours over the years struggling to find her purpose, when it was sitting right in front of her.*

》 What have you always found easy?

The question is—what comes easy for you? *Easy* doesn't mean it's literally a piece of cake, but like Kathleen, it's natural, you "get it," and you thrive on it.

I hate writing. I love having written.
—Dorothy Parker, writer and satirist

In a similar way, writing comes easy for me. That's not to say that serious writing isn't an agonizing process, and I'm not sweating every word at this very moment. But the truth is, particularly when it comes to ad copy, TV commercials, promotional material, and many other projects, I can sit down and knock it out while other people are still thinking. I can't explain it, but I have a knack for it. And even when it's tough, I still love doing it—especially after it's finished.

I'll never forget filming a project in Italy many years ago. We were shooting all night on a cold, windy, and rainy hillside a couple of hours north of Rome. The crew was exhausted and we were ready to call it a night. But as I stood there next to the camera at three in the morning, fighting the freezing rain—absolutely miserable from a human perspective—the thought occurred to me that I was having the time of my life.

Think about your life. How many times were you asked to do something because you were the organized one, the athletic one, the good writer, or the most patient? Perhaps you're the responsible one who's always expected to keep your group together at the shopping mall. Perhaps you're the person everyone turns to in a crisis.

Looking back, think about the moments when you naturally gravitated toward a particular task on the homecoming committee, at church, a school project, or at the office. Sometimes you will even build a reputation as the person who finds this or that task, project, or challenge easier than anyone else.

Far too often we simply brush these compliments aside, when they could be a critical key to our future calling.

Start today considering what comes easy in your life. As I mentioned before it's not that it's without effort or pain, but it's so natural you do it better than most people without even thinking.

It's not necessarily a role or job, but it could be. For instance, it could be coaching, writing, managing a project, teaching, or being brilliant in the kitchen.

But for most people and in most cases, the "thing" is an ability, a skill, a God-given capacity to handle something other people find challenging. Something bigger than a single job that could apply to many fields, such as the uncanny ability to sense when others are hurting, the knack for motivating people in difficult circumstances, or the talent for leadership.

Don't guess, and don't make a snap judgment. Take your time, and really think about the possibilities.

DO OTHER PEOPLE CONFIRM IT?

One of the reasons Kathleen is constantly asked to organize projects and events is that other people see her success. Her talent is confirmed in the eyes of outsiders.

What have you done that made people notice? What brings you affirmation, encouragement, and compliments from friends and coworkers? Generally speaking, people can be harsh, so when you do get an encouraging word—especially from people who you don't normally expect it from—you should notice. Because it may be pointing in the direction of your one thing.

Outside confirmation is not just about encouragement, it's about acknowledging excellence. Recently, I met an actor here in Hollywood who is passionate and driven, and his goal is to be a great actor. But my new friend has one simple problem: he's terrible at it. I viewed some scenes he's done in a few low-budget films and commercials, and it doesn't take an expert to see that he has no technique, little talent, and a tin ear for dialogue.

The problem is, acting is all he's wanted to do since high school. He left the Midwest a decade ago and moved to Hollywood to pursue the dream. He refuses to get a full-time job so he'll have plenty of time for auditions, so he lives in cheap, dangerous neighborhoods and gets by on food stamps. His single-minded pursuit has cost him his family—his wife left him and took their son back to their hometown because of their financial struggles.

But he considers that collateral damage in pursuit of his art.

He receives no confirmation of his talent because he has none. But he continues forward because he refuses to be brutally honest about his ability—or lack thereof.

There are many things I love to do, but my lack of talent in those areas keeps me from seriously considering them as a potential OBT. Paying attention to outside confirmation of your gifts and abilities from your peers is an important guidepost on the journey to your One Big Thing.

> ## A critic is the man who knows the way, but can't drive a car.
> —Kenneth Tynan, writer and theater critic

While outside *confirmation* is a good thing, outside *criticism* needs to be handled with care. My advice is to weigh any outside influence in the balance of who and how qualified they are. While your writing teacher, business mentor, or experienced friend should be listened to and their advice acted on, keep in mind that coworkers and family members sometimes operate out of jealousy or ignorance. When your writing teacher recommends you keep the day job until you improve your writing, that's worth listening to. But when your neighbor criticizes your decision because she thinks you need a "real" job, then keep moving forward.

Too many dreams are ended because someone listened to the wrong person. I have friends whose advice and counsel I value, and other friends (whom I love just as dearly) I never listen to when it comes to my dream or career.

Know the difference.

To fly we have to have resistance.
—Maya Lin, sculptor

It's worth taking a moment and mentioning how to deal with criticism, because it can so easily derail the search for your one thing. Here are a few important tips:

1. Take it.

Don't be defensive and fire back. Listen and learn. It may be completely ridiculous, but even the worst critics sometimes stumble onto a grain of truth. My opinion is that we can always learn and grow, so never shut the door on a critic too quickly.

I know a religious leader who was hurt by a close friend early in his career so he decided to shut the door on all criticism. He doesn't read stories about himself in the newspaper, doesn't want to hear what outsiders are saying, and doesn't allow the staff to criticize his ideas. Over the years he's become smaller and smaller, and today lives in a bubble of his own making. He never heard valuable criticism he could have benefited from, and as a result his life and career have been stunted.

So even though you may think it's unfair (and it may well be), take it. Listen to the critic and see if there's anything there worth changing.

2. Admit your mistakes.

Nothing so surprises and disarms a critic like someone who agrees with him or her. If it's good criticism, your admission is appropriate and welcomed. Even if it's not good criticism, then you've taken away his or her ammunition. Man up. Don't argue. Just say thank you and move on.

When it comes to mistakes, I'm surprised that political candidates still think they can hide their past. Whatever the problem—a past sexual affair, financial mistake, or poor decision—the best thing is to get it out there first. In a digital world, you can't hide your past, so being the first to deal with it publicaly greatly diffuses future criticism.

Likewise, in most situations, graciously accepting criticism usually catches the critic offguard and in many cases, silences him or her forever.

3. Gently explain the reasons for your action.

I have a quote from Plato on my computer desktop: "Be kind, for everyone you meet is fighting a hard battle." Sometimes we mess up, don't know what the other person is going through, and simply make mistakes in judgment. On the flip side, the critics don't know everything behind your actions either. So without being defensive, explain yourself. It's not about rationalizing or explaining away the criticism, but informing the critic of what you were thinking. In many cases, once he or she realizes your motivation, the comment will be dropped.

Far too many people can't discern the confirmation of their gifts in the eyes of other people because they're so overly sensitive to criticism. As a result, they overreact and are defensive to everything. I honestly believe some people spend their lives waiting to be offended.

Get over it. It's not about you. Have the confidence to accept compliments and criticism equally. Doing so will completely change how others see you and help you weather life's real storms.

> **》 For many people, accepting compliments is just as challenging as accepting criticism.**

I have spoken at events at which I was surprised by the emotional outpouring of many in the audience. I'll be at a book signing and afterward someone will walk up in tears and describe how one of my books has made a major impact on his or her life. In some cases, after reading the book, people have found the courage to leave a dead-end job or start a new business or career. These are life-changing stories.

The first time it happened, I felt awkward and deflected the compliments. Then I realized this person really needed to share his story, and if I failed to accept the compliment I was belittling his experience. Honestly, I still feel a little awkward that something I write could have that kind of effect on someone, but these people honor me with the encouragement, and I honor them by accepting the compliment, and enjoy the moment.

> **》 Let people pat you on the back occasionally. They need to say it as much as you need to hear it.**

Some people are their own worst enemy. They never receive any encouragement because, out of awkwardness or embarrassment, they won't allow people to compliment them.

Once you've learned to have an appropriate response to both criticism and compliments, you'll be in a better position to objectively evaluate the confirmation of others. That's important, because outside confirmation is a key step toward finding your One Big Thing.

> ## I was lucky—I found what I loved to do early in life.
> —Steve Jobs, cofounder of Apple

QUESTION #2: WHAT DO YOU LOVE?

Another important signpost on your journey to your OBT is discovering a task, job, purpose, or cause that you love. Some people think that's a ridiculous notion because to them, *work is work*—period. They've never felt that work was anything to enjoy, let alone love; it's only something done for a paycheck. They love what they do *after* work. But the most productive, well-rounded, and fulfilled people have found a job they love to do and do extraordinarily well.

One of the greatest tests to find out whether people truly love what they do is whether or not they'd do it without being paid. What do you love to do so badly that you'd be willing to get another job on the side so you could actually make a living? Let's face it—how many tax accountants love the job so much that if they had to do it for free, they'd work at Starbucks on the side just to make a living? (If you're passionate about being a tax accountant, my apologies.)

In all seriousness, I know my accountant loves his work because he's very analytical, loves numbers, and is incredibly grateful that those gifts make it possible to own a home, take vacations, and raise a wonderful family. From my perspective (as a creative person), just looking at a tax form horrifies me. But that's the miracle of discovering your One Big Thing—it's the ultimate expression of your individual gifts, passions, and purpose.

I have the opportunity to see many successful executives living out their passion through nonprofit and humanitarian work. They've spent their career making money—often at jobs they hated doing—and now they have the opportunity to find fulfillment helping a great and worthy cause. Becoming wealthy is a wonderful thing, but there are plenty of affluent people who are rich and miserable.

On the other hand I know men and women who have dedicated their lives to working in Third World countries. They have very little in the way of material things, but they can't wait to get up in the morning and pursue their passion.

Certainly they have challenges. Just because you're passionate about your work doesn't make it stress-free. I'm sure while she was working in the desperate slums of Calcutta, Mother Teresa thought many times about giving up and walking away. But it was her incredible love for the outcasts and lepers in India that motivated her to keep going, and her life and ideals have transformed millions of people around the world.

>> **The question is—what if you could find the intersection of those two markers: making money and fulfilling your passion?**

There are plenty of people volunteering at jobs they love and working on the side to make a living. But what if you could combine the two? What if you could actually make a living working at a job you love? If you consider the whole working world, only a tiny minority of people are actually doing a job they're passionate about.

What about you?

Here are some key questions to help you move toward actually getting paid to do what you love:

What are you willing to risk?

Depending on your age and your circumstances, you might have to make some serious changes in your life. Are you willing to downsize your lifestyle for a period to make that transition? In many cases you can actually make *more* money doing something you love, but when you love it, money isn't the only point. Everybody *talks* about pursuing their dreams, but very few are willing to risk much to make that dream happen.

One of the saddest situations I encounter is people who trade doing what they love for making a bigger paycheck. I understand seasons of life when it's necessary to put the kids through college or cover some other significant expense. Single moms have especially difficult challenges here. But the problem is that those jobs tend to suck us in and never let go.

In college, a friend and I took all the same film classes and had the same goals for a career in entertainment and media. Together we were going to conquer Hollywood. After graduation, I left for Los Angeles and he decided to take a "temporary" job at an insurance agency to pay off some debt. Months went by, and then years. I would call and ask when he was leaving the agency, but he always had a reason to stay on—a raise, a promotion, an award.

Guess what? Today he's still selling insurance. He spent his entire adult life at a job he didn't particularly like because of his desire to make more money. The regret is evident in every phone call and e-mail message. He traded his dream for a bigger paycheck.

If only. Those must be the two saddest words in the world.

—Mercedes Lackey, author

I have an attorney friend who's had an incredibly successful career as a corporate attorney, but is now downsizing his life to pursue his dream of international social justice. Obviously an attorney representing America's most successful corporations makes more money than the same attorney representing a victim of sex trafficking in Eastern Europe. The income may not be the same, but my friend is more excited and fulfilled than at any time in his career.

Becoming comfortable may be the greatest enemy of your life's dream, so decide what you're willing to risk and that will help determine your level of commitment.

But don't end there. Remember that many people are wealthy doing what they love. Whether it's filmmaking, writing, performing, banking, coaching, or whatever—they've discovered a passion that rewards them financially. But keep in mind that in the beginning, it might be years before your financial goals are realized. We all know the successful writer who started out as a starving artist, or the NCAA national championship coach who began as an assistant coach at a losing high school.

The questions are—what are you willing to risk and for how long?

Everyone is passionate about something. It's your job to find out what it is.

—Guy Kawasaki, author of *Enchantment: The Art of Changing Hearts, Minds, and Actions*

Identify your obsession.

What are you fanatical about? I'm not talking obsession in the same sense as a psychological disorder. (Well, maybe.) In other words, what are you constantly thinking about? What type of books do you buy or television programs do you watch? What's the first thing you think about when you wake up in the morning and the last thing you think about when you go to bed at night?

» Some people live their entire lives and never connect their obsession to an actual job.

Over the years I've worked with a lot of pastors, helping each one build a media platform for extending his or her message to the world. In many cases, the pastor has never considered the idea of One Big Thing, because a typical church leader deals with such a variety of issues. Most pastors have to preach on an incredible range of subjects; they marry couples, bury the dead, manage the church, counsel struggling church members, teach classes, supervise the youth, and much more.

Focusing on one thing—especially One Big Thing—may be the hardest challenge a pastor has ever faced.

Preaching on a wide variety of subjects in church is fine, but when the pastor wants to write a book, become an outside speaker, create a study series, or produce media programming, he or she needs to *focus*. When it comes to getting his or her message noticed *outside* the local congregation, my questions to these pastors are: *What really drives you? What's the subject that you're so passionate about, you could potentially be one of the best in the world on that issue?*

> **Depend upon it, sir, when a man knows he is to be hanged in a fortnight, it concentrates his mind wonderfully.**
>
> —Samuel Johnson, eighteenth-century English writer

Perhaps more graphically: *If I held a gun to your head and said you could only write or preach on one subject for the rest of your life, what would that subject be?*

That's a question all of us should answer. Pastors, CEOs, teachers, filmmakers, writers, business leaders, real estate agents, sales professionals, and more: *If I held a gun to your head and said you could only do one thing for the rest of your life, what would it be?*

It's a question of *filters*. In other words, a pastor doesn't have to stop preaching on a wide variety of subjects. A filmmaker doesn't have to stop creating movies on the subjects that fascinate him. A business leader doesn't have to stop buying, selling, or leading different types of companies. But discovering your passion or obsession (your OBT) becomes a filter that everything else passes through.

For more than twenty years, until his retirement from the church to lead the King's University, Jack Hayford was our family's pastor at the Church on the Way, in Van Nuys, California. Over those years I've heard Jack preach on everything you can imagine—Scriptures, Bible stories, family challenges, world events, and much more. I've probably heard nearly a thousand messages from "Pastor Jack." But you don't listen to Jack long before you realize his real passion is *worship*. He's written books on the subject and composed more than one hundred worship songs. During all those years, he even led the congregation in worship along with preaching the Sunday sermon.

The bottom line is that whatever he preaches, writes, or composes—Jack Hayford does it through the lens of *worship*. Worship acts as a filter that everything passes through. So whatever he preaches on—stories like David and Goliath, the death and resurrection of Jesus, reaching out to the poor and needy, or what the Bible says about families—is viewed through the perspective of *worship*.

Understanding that principle changes everything. As a result of Jack's passion for worship, his teaching cuts through the clutter and gets noticed. His expertise, insight, and passion for that subject has made Jack known throughout the world and he has impacted millions of lives.

Although he's brilliant at a wide variety of subjects and issues—and they all contribute to who he is—Jack Hayford's legacy won't be his teaching on Bible prophecy, church administration, or doctrine. He'll be remembered for what he taught today's church about *worship*.

When it comes to his OBT, Jack Hayford has figured it out. Identifying it and understanding how to follow it are critical steps in the realization of yours.

Is your filter social justice? Then you can write books, speak at conferences, make films, and more, while filtering those projects through the lens of social justice.

Entrepreneur Guy Kawasaki was one of the early employees at Apple Computer, but it wasn't long before he took his zeal for the Mac into other areas as well. Guy's filter is *empowering people*, and he does that through personal conversations, a blog, writing books, public speaking, and more. His OBT doesn't limit him; in fact, it allows him to expand his influence to reach far more people with his unique message.

But wait—a lot of people are good at "empowering others." What makes Guy's message unique?

Guy's background at Apple, his experience as an early evangelist for the Mac, his engaging personality, his perspective on issues like world travel and spirituality, his love of discovery, his gift for writing, and more—all contribute to a unique take on empowering people. Plenty of others may be good at empowering or encouraging, but nobody does it in the exact same way as Guy, and that's why people are so eager to read his books, hear him speak, and learn from his message.

Understand that value matters.

Pursuing your passion as a job may mean you start doing it for free. At one time in her career, my wife, Kathleen, managed the internship program for the film students at Biola University here in Los Angeles. Her job was to help these young film students get an internship at a major Hollywood movie studio, production company, or television network. Working with a top-notch faculty, the program gained a widely respected reputation. As a result of the quality of students, the program typically had more intern requests from studios than she could fill.

These students were willing to work for free because they had little experience, limited skill, and were new to the industry. They were willing to get sandwiches or coffee and make script copies just to get in the door of a major studio. In a gratifying number of cases, those free internships resulted in full-time jobs and open doors into the industry.

In the pursuit of finding a job that connects to your passion, you may want to consider working as a free intern. Especially if you're a college student with limited experience and knowledge about the endeavor, I think it's a wise choice. If you're an older worker, perhaps offering free time to assist a more experienced mentor would give you an extraordinary look into a different business or industry.

However, don't get stuck in that thinking.

>> **The key is determining the intersection between what you're passionate about and what people are willing to pay you to do it.**

In consulting with nonprofit clients, our company, Cooke Pictures, gets a lot of requests to do pro bono (or free) work. After all, there are many great nonprofit organizations out there with a powerful mission but little or no budget. We're always happy to help when we can, and I schedule meetings regularly with various leaders of small nonprofits to give them advice at no charge.

There's a catch-22 though. Our primary strength is to help an entity share its story through the media—but much of the cost of defining a brand, producing television or online content, building a website, buying radio or TV time, or placing other media and advertising is out of our hands. Media buying isn't cheap, frankly, thus the hard costs of any project can be an expensive proposition.

So I've become more and more firm about my fees. Not because I'm a money-grubbing jerk, but because I've discovered that it's a good benchmark to determine just how serious my clients are about what it will take. After all, if they can't pay my fee for a meeting or our retainer for continuing consultation, then they certainly can't afford to be on radio, TV, or other media platforms.

In my case, it's helped weed out many organizations that have wonderful intentions and are staffed by good people but don't really have the financial resources or the commitment to see the vision through when the rubber meets the road. As a result, we can focus more of our time with those clients who do have the resources, realistic expectations, and passion to move forward.

Something to remember is that our company has been in business since 1991, and I've done this personally for more than thirty-five years. So when it comes to helping clients share a message in a media-driven world, we've developed a solid reputation and built significant relationships. As a result, we have the brand equity to set the bar higher than someone without that experience or track record.

So the key becomes what you bring to the table. And don't shortchange yourself because the job is your passion. Anytime you can give your time and energy to a great cause or a job, that's a wonderful thing. But if you're bringing significant experience, insight, and expertise to the job, then aim high and negotiate from there.

Your potential clients, investors, or donors need to see you're serious about what you're doing with your life. But only you can give them that sense of confidence. There's an adage in marketing that says when you give something away for free, that's the value people often place on it. Working for free at the *right* time can really help your career, while doing the same thing at the *wrong* time or place only hurts it.

It's a delicate balancing act—wanting to move into your dream and yet wanting to be paid to do it. But with sensitivity, you can make it happen.

Own the role.

Once you make the decision to make the move toward your OBT, immediately consider yourself in that role. If you decide to follow your passion and become a novelist, start calling yourself a novelist. Whatever your decision—entrepreneur, pastry chef, filmmaker, football coach, programmer, architect—own the role and start calling yourself by that term.

The reason is if *you* don't see yourself as a writer, coach, chef, or designer, no one else will either. *You* dictate the terms and schedule of your dream. Even if you're not making a penny or don't have a desk, office, or business card—*become that person*. Own the dream and stop being embarrassed that you don't conform to your friends' or coworkers' expectations.

Names matter, and calling yourself by your role instills confidence not only in you but in potential investors, backers, or donors. You may not have a published novel, but if you've started writing one, you're a novelist. It's no different for a filmmaker, an artist, or a businessperson. All you may have is your dream, but if you're moving forward and taking concrete steps to make that dream a reality, then you need to own it.

THE ARGUMENT AGAINST PURSUING YOUR PASSION FOR A LIVING

Some people—artists in particular—actually frown upon trying to connect their passion to their daily, paid work. The theory is you shouldn't mix your art and work because it dilutes both (especially early in the process). For instance, some recommend that if you're a writer dreaming of becoming a novelist, don't get a day job as an advertising or technical writer. The belief is that at the end of the day you'll come home worn out from writing all day and the last thing you'll want to do is work on your novel.

This line of thinking maintains the goal is to do something as far from your dream as possible. After flipping burgers or selling insurance all day, you'll come home sick of a normal job and dive into your real passion. An artist who dreams of a career as a serious portrait painter shouldn't get a day job as a graphic designer for the same reason.

I think there's some truth to this idea, but it's really a question of the individual person and situation. I've personally worked with numerous TV commercial directors who started out with the dream of directing feature films. But they started to like the money and awards of a commercial career, so they eventually put their feature film plans permanently on the shelf. Right or wrong, it's something they have to decide for themselves.

I also know incredibly talented artists who neglected their art while moving up the ladder as graphic designers in the advertising industry. They became so focused on winning awards and impressing clients in the ad business, they had little time or energy left at the end of the day to create the art they dreamed of.

On the other hand, many talented artists mix the two, and become internationally known as award-winning graphic, product, or industrial designers. A perfect example is Yves Béhar, an industrial designer who in 1999 founded fuseproject, a San Francisco–based design and branding agency. Béhar poured his artistic gifts into making a global impact designing products and communication strategies that have won numerous international awards. He feels that his design work for corporate clients *is* his real art, and pours every inch of his formidable talent into each project.

Whether producing corporate videos inspires you to keep working on a feature film, or writing greeting cards by day inspires your novel by night—that's something only you can decide. Or you can mix them both to become an award-winning commercial director, graphic designer, ghostwriter, or consultant. You're the only person who can decide what works for you.

DOING WHAT YOU LOVE HELPS YOU THROUGH THE DIFFICULT TIMES

Perhaps most important, a deep love for your work can get you through the failures, the difficulties, and the times when you're ready to give up. That's what happened when Steve Jobs was fired from Apple Computer, the company he cofounded in 1984. Here's the way he described it in the address he gave to the 2005 graduating class of Stanford University:

> I'm convinced that the only thing that kept me going was that I loved what I did. You've got to find what you love. And that is as true for your work as it is for your lovers. Your work is going to fill a large part of your life, and the only way to be truly satisfied is to do what you believe is great work. And the only way to do great work is to love what you do. If you haven't found it yet, keep looking. Don't settle. As with all matters of the heart, you'll know when you find it. And, like any great relationship, it just gets better and better as the years roll on. So keep looking until you find it. Don't settle.

Steve Jobs faced plenty of obstacles over the years, including being driven out of the very company he cofounded. He could have easily given up and walked away. You and I face challenges on a regular basis that make us wonder if it's time to pack it up and forget about the dream. But the power of the dream keeps pulling us back. It's something we love—something we can't live without.

Don't tell my agent or publisher, but if I had to, I'd write for free. Writing my blog has saved me thousands on therapy; writing my books has helped me work through some of the most difficult questions I've ever faced. It's what keeps me coming back to the keyboard.

Find what you love, and it will make a powerful difference during the struggle of your daily living.

QUESTION #3: WHAT DRIVES YOU CRAZY?

I've discovered that in many cases, the thing you hate the most could be the problem you were born to fix. In other words, what do you hate? What drives you nuts? I believe the key to your destiny could be found in the answer to those questions.

I have a friend who hated stories of young girls who became pregnant out of wedlock and were suddenly dumped by their boyfriend or family, stories about girls in love who heard that tired phrase, "If you *really* loved me . . ." and felt the enormous pressure to begin having sex as the only way to stay in a relationship. But once they discovered they were pregnant, all that professed love from the boyfriend evaporated. The next thing they knew the boyfriend was gone, the family had abandoned them, and they were left to have an abortion or go to term, at which point they'd either give up the baby for adoption or raise the child—all alone.

Those stories of girls being abandoned made my friend crazy. They simply drove her nuts. So she decided to do something about it. Through her sheer drive and determination, she's created a network of homes literally around the world that takes these desperate women in, helps them finish high school or college, trains them for a job, gets them back on their feet, and helps them raise the child or find a good home with loving parents to adopt.

It started small and took years to grow, but today she's impacting young women around the world and giving them a second chance at life.

It didn't come about from passion, a gift, a talent, or even a passing interest.

It all started with something that drove her crazy.

Another friend, Christine Caine, would get physically ill hearing stories of women trafficked globally for sex. Learning that they were kidnapped, drugged, moved in packed shipping containers from port to port, and then forced into a life of drug addiction and sex with strangers, Christine often broke down in tears when she heard about the incredible evil of the sex industry.

That's when Christine and her husband, Nick, formed the A21 Campaign to do something about it. They don't claim to be experts; and they recognize the fight for justice for these women has only just begun. But by building rescue shelters throughout Europe, providing medical care, and helping them piece their shattered lives together, this remarkable couple is making a dramatic difference for women on a global basis.

"Never doubt that a small group of thoughtful committed people can change the world. Indeed, it is the only thing that ever has." It's not known who said that—but the A21 Campaign embodies the spirit and determination conveyed in the message. Even one person can make a significant change in the world. Christine and Nick Caine didn't have any money or an organization behind them, but today they're making a global difference. And it all began with discovering something they hated. Something that drove them nuts.

It doesn't have to be a social cause. It could be something you hate about your mobile phone, the industrial process at work, your schedule, public education, or the structure of your company. It could be your inability to find a certain product, or the absence of a solution to a pressing social issue.

How often have you asked: "Why isn't there a _____?" Whatever it is, think about it, isolate it, and realize that fixing that issue could be what you've been put on the earth to accomplish.

> **Think of what frustrates you—and if you're frustrated by something and you feel "Dammit, if only people could do this better," then go try to do it better yourself. It can start off in a really small way . . . and you'll be surprised: If you're doing it better yourself, in whatever field it is, you'll be filling a gap and you suddenly might start creating a business.**
> **—Richard Branson, founder of Virgin Airways**

A few years ago I helped lead a workshop at the Sundance Film Festival in Utah and spoke about starting the search for your OBT with something that drives you crazy. One of the students came up to me the next day and said, "I've been wrestling with my purpose in life for years. I'm in graduate school, but just can't decide where I can make a difference or what I'm passionate about. But after your lecture, I went to my room and made a list of four things I really hated, and discovered that all four came from essentially the same cause. At that moment, it was like a window opened, and I discovered what I was born to do."

Some of the greatest causes in the history of the world have been driven by injustice. The civil rights movement was inspired by a dream, but was driven by the burning desire to right an injustice. Sometimes it's enough to see a wrong and invest your life into making it right.

Try it yourself. What do you hate? What drives you nuts in life? The answer may change the course of your future.

**Eighty percent of success
is just showing up.**

—Woody Allen, filmmaker

Remember, it doesn't matter what your job is right now or what you do for a living. The answer to what frustrates you could express itself in a new product, an original method, a movie, a book, a march, a campaign, a cause, or a religious awakening. It doesn't have to be big, it just needs to start.

You just need to show up.

COULD IT BE SOMETHING YOU'RE WRESTLING WITH RIGHT NOW?

I don't write books because I have all the answers. I write books because I'm struggling with the questions and searching for solutions. The story of my blog at philcooke.com is simply the story of my daily journey looking for answers to challenges and frustrations I encounter helping people and organizations tell their story.

**We should learn from the mistakes
of others. We don't have time to
make them all ourselves.**

—Groucho Marx, comedian and film star

I think if they're honest, most writers, filmmakers, and other artists would tell you something similar. Every day we encounter challenges and every day we have the chance to work through them.

Very often, those challenges are the key to discovering our One Big Thing.

If you attend church regularly you've probably seen it played out on a weekly basis in your pastor's sermons. A very interesting thing I remember about one particular evangelist's sexual affair and fall from grace in the eighties was that for years he had been preaching about *sexual sin*. And it wasn't just occasionally. In reviewing his catalog of sermons from the time, I was surprised at how often he preached on that subject. I met another TV evangelist one time right before his financial and sexual scandal went public, and guess what he wanted to talk about? You guessed it—he was joking about sex.

It wasn't long before his sexual double life surfaced.

More recently, our company considered working with a successful pastor in Europe. Whenever I met with him, all he wanted to talk about was his "beautiful family." At first I was impressed that he put such a value on wife and kids, but after awhile it become too much. Over and over he would point out how great his wife looked, and how important sex was to their life. I thought it a bit weird and over the top at the time.

A few months later, he was arrested for having sex with multiple women in his congregation.

I've been a church member all my life. And in my experience one thing you can almost always count on is this: pastors work out their own personal demons in the sermons they preach. Good or bad, whatever they're wrestling with inside will work its way out in their messages. I've discovered over the years that when a preacher hammers away on a particular subject—sexual immorality, financial issues, family, or whatever—it's a good indication of what he or she is struggling with personally.

And it's worth noting that the flip side is just as consistent. Hundreds of thousands of pastors and church leaders around the world are doing honorable work, changing lives in desperate situations. But in the same way, even these great challenges are being worked through in the sermons they preach.

The bottom line?

WHATEVER WE'RE WRESTLING WITH PERSONALLY COMES OUT IN OUR WORK

You may not be in a traditionally creative job, one in which you can write, preach, make films, or create art. But trust me, your struggles will manifest themselves in the quality of work you're doing.

Take notice. Take notice of the types of projects you request at work. Take notice of the books you buy, the movies you see, and the TV programs you view. Take notice of the types of friends you have, the conferences you attend, and your magazine subscriptions.

While it's certainly not true in all cases, your daily decisions are a window into your struggles, your passions, and your dreams.

What you buy and how you live your life reveals more about you than you realize.

QUESTION #4: WHAT DO YOU WANT TO LEAVE BEHIND?

I can't remember the TV commercial, but I'll never forget a line from the script: "Nobody is remembered for being *almost* famous."

We all want to be remembered, and when it comes to leaving a legacy, we rarely recall people who were pretty good at a lot of things.

> ## Show me your checkbook, and
> ## I'll show you your priorities.
> **—Larry Burkett, financial expert
> and radio personality**

When bicycles became the new sensation in the late nineteenth century, two brothers named Orville and Wilbur Wright started a company called the Wright Cycle Exchange, which later became the Wright Cycle Company. They were so successful, they started manufacturing their own brand of bikes in 1896. Talented in numerous areas, they had previously owned a printing press and over the years worked with motors and other machines.

But when it comes to legacy, what do people remember about the Wright brothers? (Hint: it's not the bicycle they designed that today is on display at the National Air and Space Museum.) Instead, they recall that long stretch of sand in Kitty Hawk, North Carolina, where on December 17, 1903, Orville and Wilbur beat the law of gravity and flew the first successful airplane.

Henry Ford was an expert watch repairman by age fifteen, later an apprentice machinist, a steam engine operator, and eventually trained in bookkeeping. But the only people who remember his skills in those areas are a handful of historians, while the rest of us can never forget his invention of the automobile.

It's hard enough being remembered at all, but focusing on One Big Thing is the key to a lasting legacy.

What is it you want to leave behind? What do you want to be remembered for?

Now, go back, take some time, and review these four important questions:

1. What comes easy for you?
2. What do you love?
3. What drives you crazy?
4. What do you want to leave behind?

Using that matrix, you should start zeroing in on what that illusive OBT is in your life.

Now the question becomes, *How do you get that story out there?* Or as Steve Jobs would have asked, *How do you make a dent in the universe?*

Chapter Nine

BECOME A FORCE TO BE RECKONED WITH

Getting Your Story Out There

Every story you tell is your own story.

—JOSEPH CAMPBELL, MYTHOLOGIST, WRITER, AND LECTURER

There is no agony like bearing an untold story inside you.

—MAYA ANGELOU, POET

As we've seen, getting your story told in a digital culture is tough. The demands, options, and choices your audience faces today are daunting. I was a partner in a television commercial company during one of the most chaotic and disruptive times in the history of the advertising business. During the last decade, in spite of producing two Super Bowl commercials and many national campaigns for major companies, every new pitch for business was still a challenge. Competition from the Internet has forever damaged the business of thirty-second TV commercials, and while the spot format won't go away anytime soon, it's facing a watershed moment.

As a result, with every media platform we're constantly innovating and brainstorming new ways to reach consumers with our client's message. If they're not watching TV, where can we find them? If they're on the Web, how do we compete against billions of websites for their attention? What role should social media play in building that message?

The questions go on and on, because in a digital culture only the messages that actually *connect* will make an impact.

From that experience, I've discovered some important insights to unlocking the puzzle. To get your message heard, these are the elements that most often need to be in place to be successful:

1. THE POWER OF ORIGINALITY

**To be original, seek your inspiration
from unexpected sources.**

—Paul Arden, from his book *It's Not How Good
You Are, It's How Good You Want to Be*

In a sea of competition, the quickest way to get noticed is to be completely original. Apple Computer got it right when they launched the "Think Different" campaign. In a world of interchangeable ideas, cloned products, and tribal thinking, we desperately long for something new.

As cartoonist and artist Hugh MacLeod says, "The idea doesn't have to be big. It just has to be yours." Stop trying to be like someone else and start looking deep into your life for what makes your message, story, or project unique and different. What does your unique background, education, gifts and talents, life experience, and values say about the originality of your message?

Part of what gives Flannery O'Conner's stories a unique voice is the fact that she raised chickens on a farm in Milledgeville, Georgia. Had she lived in New York City or London, how different would her perspective on writing and life have been?

Ernest Hemingway loved adventure, and his book, *A Moveable Feast,* opens a wonderful curtain to the imaginative period during which he lived in Paris.

How did Sergey Brin's childhood in Russia inform his development of "search" and lead him to cofound a company called Google?

What drove Mother Teresa to the slums of Calcutta or Martin Luther King Jr. to the forefront of the civil rights movement?

What were the personal and spiritual values that made John Wooden one of the greatest basketball coaches in history?

I'm currently reading historian David McCullough's book, *The Greater Journey,* about the adventurous writers, doctors, inventors, artists, politicians, architects, and others who set off for Paris between 1830 and 1900—because during that period Paris was such a creative and stimulating city. The book traces the incredible impact that experience had on their lives and work.

» What about your life and experience gives you a unique and original perspective?

But consider the flip side of originality. University professors across the country and around the world are brilliant at their area of expertise, and yet the vast majority of academic journals encourage readers to do little more than yawn. Leaders in C-suites are rarely more than filling a role. How often do you actually encounter a business leader with a remarkable and original vision? Tens of thousands of pastors across the country bring a myriad of life experience, knowledge, and perspectives into their work, and yet the vast majority of their books and sermons are average at best.

What's the point? *Original thinking* changes everything.

Certainly it's natural to want to mimic and copy. Hollywood has built a global business on producing sequels. As I write this, Michael Bay's third version of the movie *Transformers* is hitting theaters and looks to be a great success. If you can generate that much money making sequels, it's understandable why Hollywood invests so much money in franchise properties.

The book industry has followed that lead. I saw a best-selling book recently that's spawned a version for teens, another version for moms, a calendar, a daily devotional, and a study series for small groups—not to mention coffee cups and T-shirts.

But there's no question that all those sequels and ancillary products began with an *original idea*.

> **Ideas can be life-changing.**
> **Sometimes all you need to open the**
> **door is just one more good idea.**
>
> —**Jim Rohn, entrepreneur, author,**
> **motivational speaker**

We're all capable of original ideas. So many of us are convinced we're not creative that we shove our inventive impulses into the background of our lives. But take a look at young children. Every child is widely creative, yet something happens about school age that begins to fight against those artistic instincts.

I'll never forget the day when I started thinking like an adult, and I've always been a bit nostalgic about that moment. As a young boy we lived near the woods, and it wasn't unusual for me to disappear into the trees at sunrise and not return until the end of the day. My dog, Boots, and I spent my childhood reliving World War II movies—hunting German soldiers hidden deep inside the woods outside Charlotte, North Carolina.

They were all imaginary, of course, but vivid for me and Boots.

But one day we headed into the woods and I was surprised to discover that the German soldiers were gone. No matter how I tried, I could not summon them up. They refused to shoot back. They had retreated into my memory.

Over the next few days, I made other forays into the battlefield, but with no luck.

They were gone for good.

I may have matured that day, but I never let go of my imagination. It has fueled my life and work over all these years, and I refuse to give in.

You're just as creative. You may have simply given up on the journey.

A rock pile ceases to be a rock pile the moment a single man contemplates it, bearing within him the image of a cathedral.
—Antoine de Saint-Exupéry,
French writer and aviator

Dig down into your treasure chest of creativity. It may have been buried in the sands of your subconscious, but it's still there. Here are a few keys to unlocking the old chest and mining its riches:

Open yourself to other people's ideas.

Playwright George Bernard Shaw said,

> If I have an idea and give the idea away it is not gone, but I still have it! This experience does not conform to the arithmetic of things. Let us examine this experience from the point of view of exchange. If I have an apple and you have an apple and we exchange apples—then you have an apple and I have an apple. But if I have the idea that the apple is red and you have the idea that the apple is small and we exchange ideas, then you have two ideas and I have two ideas. It is quite obvious, therefore, that the laws governing thoughts or ideas are different from the laws governing things. If I have an idea and give it away, I still have it to give again, and if I give the idea away again and again, I still have the idea left. (Quoted in *Phi Kappa Phi Journal*, March 1952)

We grow from exposure to other people's ideas, so expand your reading, visit a museum, listen to opposing opinions, track trends, and put your life on a growth curve. It's never too late to learn, and expanding your educational horizons is a key step toward cultivating new ideas. If you're writing a book, read similar books—not to steal their ideas, but to see other perspectives. I learned long ago that the best ideas hit me when I'm reading books. A thought or statement will spark the connection to something I've been struggling with and the answer happens.

Write it down.

How many times has a brilliant thought struck, but before you could make a note you lost it? Ideas are the most fragile things in the world, and if you don't write them down, they'll be lost forever. I've met people who have literally made millions of dollars off ideas that—had they not written them down—would have been forgotten about completely. Once you've heard one of those stories, you'll never be caught without a notebook or mobile device again.

What do you use? I have an iPhone app that allows me to make a note that is automatically e-mailed to me. I also have apps for voice recording, to-do lists, and more. I also keep a notebook handy with plenty of pens.

Research by the Change Anything organization (changeanything.com) confirms that one of the most effective tools for change is a recording method—pen, pencil, notebook, laptop, or mobile device. Simply writing down your plan or idea increases your chance of success by almost a third! Don't let the idea that could transform your life disappear because you didn't write it down.

Inspiration happens, but the best may take time.

Rome wasn't built in a day, and life-changing ideas don't happen overnight. Don't get frustrated if you don't start writing best-selling novels right away, if your business doesn't double in sales, or if your church doesn't explode to ten thousand members overnight.

American-raised author and journalist Tatiana de Rosnay wrote the novel *Sarah's Key* in 2002. It was a dark historical story about rounding up Jews for detention and eventual deportation to the Auschwitz concentration camp. It certainly wasn't a positive story with a glowing happy ending, and was eventually rejected by more than twenty publishers.

Most writers would have become frustrated and bitter at that point, and many would have simply given up. Not Rosnay, who went back to the computer and wrote two more novels. Those were published, but sold no more than about two thousand copies each.

Obviously the signs were apparent: her career would not be as a writer.

But she refused to listen to those signs and simply never gave up. Eventually, while having lunch with a businesswoman she had profiled for a magazine article, she learned that the woman was starting a new publishing house. Rosnay pitched her original novel, and the businesswoman was interested. Two weeks later they made a deal and *Sarah's Key* was published in France, where the story is set.

To date it's sold five million copies and been released in thirty-eight countries; a movie version starring Kristen Scott Thomas has also been released.[12]

**You just can't beat the person
who never gives up.**

—Babe Ruth, baseball legend

2. UNDERSTAND THE PLATFORMS

A significant number of dreamers fail because they don't understand the *reality* of making that dream happen. I couldn't possibly count the number of screenplays that writers who know nothing about how the movie business works have pitched me. In a similar way, millions of people have mobile app ideas but no clue how they're actually produced.

» Understand the business.

The last thing most of us creative types want to do is learn the *business* of anything. I want to create, and I've spent my adult career looking for a business partner to help me navigate the media industry. I've learned I won't get very far if I don't know how to make my creative dreams work in the real world.

Knowing how the publishing industry works won't compromise your original idea, and it might open you up to insights about the marketplace and how to sell more books. The movie business isn't much different. Lots of wannabe film producers and directors exist across the country and around the world. But how many have actually taken the time and made the effort to learn development, production, and distribution? Could having an agent help or hurt? What about a personal manager? Should I protect my ideas legally? There are a host of questions that need to be answered before anyone will seriously consider your idea.

In business, where are the conferences and seminars that would allow you to have a platform for your ideas? I'm involved on the planning teams for a number of major conferences, and I'm always astonished at the number of people who call me up a week before an event asking to speak. They may have something important to share, but don't realize speaker schedules are locked in months—and sometimes years—before these events. Because they haven't taken the time to learn how the business works, they don't have a voice.

> **There is no such thing as bad publicity except your own obituary.**
> —**Brendan Behan, Irish poet, playwright, and novelist**

The public relations industry is a great example of a business that has changed dramatically in recent years. A decade ago, people sent out press releases by the dozens.

Someone gets a promotion—a press release goes out.

You acquire a new company—a press release goes out.

The company records record sales—a press release goes out.

They used to be mailed, then faxed, then e-mailed—and when the press release went digital, it became a flood. As a result, classic press releases have very little of the impact they once did. I observed a major organization recently that launched a classic press release about a legal issue in which the company was involved. It fell flat. I tracked it on the Web, and as far as I could see, only three news outlets even posted it.

The organization this company was fighting took a different approach. They blogged about it, because they had tens of thousands of regular blog readers. Not only did it get read, but it was reposted on other blogs, sent out via social media, and numerous news organizations reported it. It probably received thousands of times the readership that the other side's classic press release received.

This isn't to say press releases are dead, but public relations professionals know that the art of getting your story out there has changed significantly.

›› In a digital world, platforms matter more than ever.

When my book *Jolt!* shipped, I didn't send out press releases. Instead I wrote articles that were tied to the subject matter of the book. As a result, those stories were picked up by major political, technology, lifestyle, and religious websites around the world. Magazines and local newspapers published the stories, and I was asked to speak at conferences based on that coverage.

Clearly, the world has changed. Is your story better told in a book, a downloadable pdf, a blog, a video presentation, a magazine article, a PowerPoint deck, a radio program, or a movie? It's not just about numbers, it's about the right audience.

I mentioned earlier that in India, my wife, Kathleen, and I spoke to a conference of young creative leaders. There were about five hundred attendees who had come from across the country to be at the event. Although I've had the opportunity to speak to tens of thousands of people around the world, I also knew five hundred creative professionals was an audience with enormous influence.

›› Stop looking for the *biggest* crowd, and start looking for the *right* crowd.

Platforms matter. As you develop your OBT, keep in mind that you'll never get the message out there until you understand the multiple platforms available. Start your education today.

Stephen King understands how the publishing industry works.

Steven Spielberg understands the movie business.

Rick Warren understands how to lead a church.

Mark Zuckerberg understands social media.

Kobe Bryant understands the business of professional basketball.

And visionaries like Richard Branson have learned how to operate on multiple platforms and extend their influence across many different brands.

All are successful not simply because they have creative ideas and strategies, but because they know the *business* of how to turn those ideas into reality.

3. LEARN THE POWER OF A NAME

In a digital, distracted culture, names matter more than ever. That's why to get your book, movie, business, or other project noticed, you need to think seriously about the name.

You've heard it before—it's all about choice. With thousands of daily choices out there, no one is going to take the time to step further in unless the name invites them.

The perfect illustration is to stand in a major bookstore. With thousands of books screaming at you from the shelf, what do you pick? Most people don't pick the one with the best story, the most profound meaning, or the most talented writer. Most pick a book that "looks interesting"—meaning the title and cover design seem like something that might fascinate them. It's only after the purchase that readers move past the title and start exploring the story.

Granted, many of us go into a bookstore having done some research into a specific book. But just as often (and probably most often for most people) books are purchased on the spur of the moment—by impulse.

It's no different with TV programs, business names, movie titles, or conference themes. I'm so passionate about this fact that I often volunteer to help create more inviting conference workshop names. There's nothing more boring than attending a workshop called "Media Inequities: Rights and Wrongs in a Post-Television Culture."

Why not change that title to "The 10 Biggest Mistakes in Media"? Trust me, it will double the attendance.

Grand Rapids Baptist College was a Christian college with a great reputation. Founded in Grand Rapids, Michigan, it was an excellent academic school.

But in 1999, they decided to take a really big step and change the name to Cornerstone University. They didn't change the faculty, the curriculum, the buildings, or the endowment. They only changed the name. But the enrollment dramatically increased in just one year.

After all, who wants to attend Grand Rapids Baptist College and Seminary? But Cornerstone University? That's a different matter.

It was already a great college, but changing the name opened the door to a far greater audience.

The right name can be a brand's most valuable asset.
—Marty Neumeier, from his book *The Brand Gap*

CBS Sunday Morning reported that years ago, the Mississippi town of Cowpens changed its name to Olive Branch. Once again, they didn't change much else, simply the name. As a result, Olive Branch, Mississippi, experienced 835 percent growth, and became the fastest-growing city in America.[13]

Don't tell me that names don't matter.

4. SPEAK THE LANGUAGE OF DESIGN

Today, we live in a design-driven generation. Visit an Apple Store, a Verizon Store, Starbucks, or look at the effort studios put into movie poster design or publishers into book cover design. This is a visual generation, and your fastest way to building a platform is to think in visual terms.

And yet I attend business meeting after business meeting and watch speakers use presentation slides filled with text. They drone on and on, thinking the slides are supporting their argument when in fact they're lulling everyone else in the room to sleep. You think your business audience will be moved more by words, or emotionally compelling images? Design is a critical part of language today, and few creative projects are produced these days without some thought of the visual.

Want to increase morale at work? Create a more inspiring visual environment.

Want to be more effective pitching your project? Learn how to tell a visual story.

Want more eyeballs for your website? Redesign it so it visually intrigues readers.

Stop taking the cheap way out by designing your own business cards.

You want to leave an impression? Think visually.

Obviously, great design isn't the entire answer. Plenty of projects that featured fantastic design have failed because of many reasons—poor funding, lack of good content, timing, and so forth.

But make no mistake. Great design is a critical component of your overall strategy. Don't leave it to chance.

5. KNOW YOUR AUDIENCE

When it comes to sharing my dream with the world, I figure out the audience first. I've found that even when I'm speaking on the same subject, how I present that subject changes dramatically depending on my audience—whether they are businesses, church groups, nonprofit organizations, conferences, colleges and universities, and so on. What I present to college students is different from what I present to business or nonprofit professionals. When it comes to getting your story heard, there is no question you need to take your audience seriously.

The digital age is about interactive communication. It's not just about sharing our message; it's about making sure the message gets heard. John Maxwell says that everybody communicates, but few connect. Our responsibility is to make sure we are connecting to our audience.

The idea of multiculturalism may be politically correct, but it simply doesn't work in real life. In fact, when it comes to communicating a message to an audience it can be damaging.

>> **While we'd all love to write books, build businesses, or make films that cross over to massive audiences, we need to begin targeting a much smaller niche.**

Audiences are dramatically different, as business leaders who travel internationally can attest. The first greeting, how you handle a business card, mobile phone etiquette, appropriate clothing—issues we in America consider fairly minor can be a major deal breaker in certain cultures.

Many years ago I was filming an outreach event in a Third World country. A large American nonprofit organization had launched a humanitarian initiative and the CEO was presenting his vision to a few hundred local business and church leaders, tribal elders, and their families. The American CEO—entirely ignorant of the audience—launched into a long joke that because of its context we immediately realized could only be understood by US audiences. Worse, it might be offensive.

However, at the end of the joke the audience roared with laughter.

Baffled, after the event I asked the translator if the audience really got the joke. He replied that like me, he recognized the story wasn't going to work, so instead of translating the speaker's actual joke, he said, while sticking to the cadence of the translation and in the local language: "The American businessman is telling a joke that you won't understand. But we want him to feel welcome. So when I give you a signal, I want all of you to laugh very loudly."

Sure enough, when the CEO hit the punch line, the translator gave the cue and the audience roared. Even today that CEO thinks he's the funniest man in the Third World.

He was saved because of the quick thinking of a translator. But you might not be so lucky. Bottom line? Respect the audience.

6. LOSE THE LINGO

This issue may not impact you at all, but I think it's worth mentioning, especially for those in academic, medical, technology, and religious situations. Certain fields today have developed their own language that people outside that world don't understand. In some cases, like medicine, it helps professionals to be more specific regarding anatomy, procedures, or diagnosis.

Inside the hospital or clinic, using these terms is a positive thing, and can make a life or death difference. But *outside* that world, it only obscures your message and damages your purpose.

I watched a couple of doctors being interviewed on the TV news after a recent tornado that devastated Joplin, Missouri. They were trying to describe the emergency care they were giving in light of the local hospital being terribly damaged by the storm. But as I sat there listening to their medical jargon, I didn't have a clue what they were talking about. Either they forgot they were speaking to the general public or didn't care. Regardless, what could have been an inspiring and encouraging message to the local community about recovering from the storm was lost in the medical lingo.

Novelist and medical doctor Michael Crichton has claimed that medical writing is a "highly skilled, calculated attempt to confuse the reader."[14] In a letter to the *New England Journal of Medicine*, a reader commented: "When do arms and legs become extremities? Why do patients ambulate, visualize, articulate and masticate when the rest of us walk, see, talk and chew? . . . Little wonder that physicians are accused of dehumanizing patients."[15]

One of the most frustrating areas when it comes to lingo is colleges and universities. When did we create a language that is only used for academic papers and research studies? We want to be precise and clear, but reading many academic journals and papers today is an exercise in obfuscation. (How's that for an academic word?) I saw a university panel recently titled: "At the Interstices:

Engaging Postcolonial and Feminist Perspectives for a Multicultural Education Pedagogy in the South." I have a PhD, and not only do I not *know* what it means, I don't *care* what it means.

What's the point? It makes you feel special. You're in a club that others can't join or understand. But one of the many problems with that thinking is that it simply limits your audience. If you're content to be read and understood only by a handful of other academics (or whoever your audience is), fine. Go for it. But if your goal is to reach the largest possible audience with your great message and purpose, then lose the lingo.

These are not flippant concerns. In an age when many more people have to work and communicate across disciplinary boundaries these things matter. In science there are excellent role models who can communicate brilliantly without in any way compromising the complexity of their ideas. That mix of confidence and clarity is a sign of intellectual energy. On the other hand we have disciplines that lack confidence and take refuge in obscurity and elitism. Perhaps this is a job for the research councils: in each discipline a prize for the best communication, and a prize for the worst deliberate obscurity. I fear that there would be no shortage of competition.[16]

—Geoff Mulgan, English writer, professor, and adviser to governments

And by the way—this goes for bad grammar as well. I'm continually stunned by the number of executives, pastors, and other leaders who make basic grammatical mistakes on a regular basis. As a communicator, language is your most important tool. Get it right or damage how you are perceived. It's as simple as that.

The power of your One Big Thing is only as effective as your ability to communicate it in today's competitive, distracted, and chaotic world. Learn to make it simple and direct. It's not about how smart you are, it's about how much your audience understands.

Chapter Ten

JUST WHEN YOU THOUGHT IT WOULD BE EASY

Challenges to Your One Big Thing

You have enemies? Good. That means you've stood up to something, sometime in your life.

—Winston Churchill, British prime minister

Adversity has the effect of eliciting talents, which in prosperous circumstances would have lain dormant.

—Quintus Horatius Flaccus (Horace), Roman lyric poet

A s you start to close in on your One Big Thing, it won't necessarily be smooth sailing. Here are some challenges you may encounter along the way:

DOES LOCATION MATTER?

Working in Hollywood, I always get the question from young film students: "Do I have to live in Los Angeles to succeed in a movie career?" My answer is that with today's technology a filmmaker can live and work anywhere. However, if you're serious about your career, you need to understand that *Hollywood is where the decisions are made.*

Certainly film projects are produced from Vancouver, Canada, to Johannesburg, South Africa. I've produced programming in both places, and forty or so other countries to boot. But unless you have all the money you need, the ultimate decisions about what script to develop, what film to green-light, the marketing and distribution strategy, and everything else, usually happens on a studio lot or network office somewhere in Los Angeles or New York City. If you're wildly successful in your career you can eventually have that ranch in Montana, and people will come to you. But for a newbie in a tough industry, there's real value in being where the decisions are made so you can be near the action.

When it comes to discovering your one thing, location matters for some people. Not because you have to be in some magical place to discover it, but because geography influences your perspective and defines the need. A political activist in Kenya is going to be presented with dramatically different issues than a similar activist in New York City. A writer in China struggles with different challenges than a writer in Paris.

For every calling or dream, geography may or may not be a factor.

» What if U2 had been born in Orange County?

Author and speaker Steve Turner wrote the brilliant book *Imagine: A Vision for Christians in the Arts*, and a few years ago I had the opportunity to meet him at a nonprofit event in Los Angeles. In our conversation, Steve brought up a brilliant point— *If the rock band U2 had been born in Orange County, California, would they have become just another church worship band?*

While not a background that would be considered traditional in America, U2's Bono was born in the north Dublin suburb of Ballymun and raised by a Catholic father and a Protestant mother—a very unique arrangement in what was, at the time, a deeply sectarian Ireland. While Bono has never been terribly outspoken about his religious faith, his lyrics, passion for social causes, and optimism in the face of global challenges have always pointed to a man who takes his faith seriously.

At the start of his music career in Ireland, Bono was already expressing his faith through his music. But there wasn't a sophisticated Christian music industry like there is in America today, so the only alternative for U2 was mainstream rock. And look at what they became. Steve's comment wasn't to slight worship bands, or dismiss explicitly Christian music, but to show how easy it is to become marginalized and derailed based on the influences of your location.

In America, Christian music has become such a significant industry it's created its own bubble. But elsewhere, that's not an option. Obviously there's a place for great music created by serious Christians, but for my money, I'm glad U2 grew up in Ireland.

Actors like New York and Los Angeles.

Political junkies prefer Washington DC.

Technology entrepreneurs like Silicon Valley.

Have you ever felt that where you're living either hurt or helped your mission in life? Have you been stunted by the lack of resources, encouragement, networks, or opportunities? On the other hand, you may live in a place where the large numbers of options are actually *detrimental* to your search. Perhaps the distractions are too great to focus on a single goal.

SURVIVING IN A DISTRACTED WORLD

I wonder if today our greatest obstacle on the road to discovering the One Big Thing is simply distractions. I'm convinced a significant number of people fail not because they aren't talented, determined, or passionate—but simply because they get distracted.

> ### It's hard to stay on purpose if we don't know what our purpose is.
> —Sam Horn, author, speaker, and consultant

Even in our daily interactions at the office we limit our ability to accomplish great things. For instance, in my experience, office interruptions are one of the major reasons we fail to achieve our goals on the job. I've never been a fan of the person who invented the "open door policy." Sure, we want to be accessible to employees and coworkers, but at some point it's time to shut the door and get to work. After your next interruption by a visitor, just make a note of how long it takes to get back to your previous level of intensity and focus. You'll be shocked at how much time that steals from your day.

Carve out time alone to focus on your dream. Many authors write books by getting up earlier in the morning and squeezing in a few hours before the phones start ringing and everyone else shows up. Others do it after the family has gone to bed. Whatever time works for you, be intentional about solitude and getting work done without distractions.

TAKE RESPONSIBILITY FOR YOUR DREAM

It's often necessary to point out that we should stop feeling guilty about creating time for our OBT; too often we allow other people's needs to come before our dream. Obviously we need to care for our children, honor our spouse, and deal with our primary responsibilities around our family or job. But the first step in achieving our dream is to take responsibility for it. That means scheduling it, and "un-scheduling" the lesser needs of our coworkers and friends. These daily commitments chip away our time, and before long it's our dream that gets lost in the shuffle.

>> **Stop doing what other people think is urgent, and start focusing on what matters to you.**

The distractions happen to everyone—from the guy at the loading dock to the secretary, to the CEO. Each of us gets pulled in different directions, but each of us has to learn to say no, whether that no is to the office party planning committee, the new corporate growth initiative, or to going out after work on Friday. If it's not a critical part of your job responsibilities or a vital role for the future of the company or your personal life, consider turning it down.

Be sensitive and respectful when you defer it, and I don't recommend you necessarily lead with "I can't be on the committee because I'm writing a best-selling novel." Don't make them envious or outright angry. In 90 percent of the cases, it's simply fine to say a gentle but firm no and tell them you have other commitments.

Practice a little and you'll gain confidence at turning down the distractions.

WHERE DOES THE WORLD'S GREAT NEED AND YOUR PASSION INTERSECT?

I'm captivated by the genesis of noble and often risky projects, and as a result, the most interesting aspect of the Invisible People website, to me, is how it was born. Having been homeless himself, founder Mark Horvath had overcome his past and worked his way back to a position as a marketing director for a large nonprofit organization. He was a born storyteller, and had the skills and talent to work for nearly any corporation or nonprofit in the country.

But the tug of the street simply wouldn't let him go. I remember discussing his future one day and mentioning that as a storyteller and former homeless person, no one knew better how to document the tragedy and triumph of families on the street. It took awhile— but when the moment of realization hit him, it was like a revelation, and Mark committed to the idea 100 percent.

From that moment on, Mark walked away from comfortable jobs and an easy life and embarked on a remarkable journey that resulted in invisiblepeople.tv—a video blog that tells the moving stories of homeless men, women, and children across the country. How he pays for it, I don't know. Were it not for the kindness of his community of friends and relationships, he would probably be homeless himself, because recording life on the street has nearly become his full-time job.

But more than that, it's become his passion. He lives and breathes his next trip, and relishes every opportunity he has to share his stories. As a result, Mark has brought together the most diverse group of people I've ever encountered. Housewives from the Midwest. Church leaders from the South. Business executives from California. He's as comfortable in a homeless shelter as he is in a boardroom. He's brought together people who would have never crossed paths had it not been for the common thread of Mark's stories.

In the process, Mark has become a real expert at using social media to generate awareness and support for causes. He's asked to speak at conferences around the world, been featured in books, magazines, and news stories, and carved out a remarkable niche as an authority on the homeless problem in America. In fact, if you ever need proof that social media can create a community, then look no further than Mark Horvath. His now multiple websites are places where thousands of people from all walks of life share pain, frustration, and hope.

Mark Horvath has found his One Big Thing.

Earlier I mentioned the saying that your ultimate goal in life should be to find the place where the world's great need and your great passion intersect. For Mark Horvath, that place is a website called invisiblepeople.tv.

The question is—*what's yours?*

Chapter Eleven

IT'S NEVER TOO LATE

The Time to Begin Is Now

If our lives are indeed the sum total of the choices that we've made, then we cannot change who we are. But with every new choice we're given, we can change who we're going to be.

—FROM *THE OUTER LIMITS* TELEVISION SHOW (1995)

The soft-minded man always fears change. He feels security in the status quo, and he has an almost morbid fear of the new. For him, the greatest pain is the pain of a new idea.

—MARTIN LUTHER KING JR., *STRENGTH TO LOVE* (1963)

I recently met an executive in his late fifties who shared with me the frustration that he had worked most of his career and yet never discovered what he was really born to do. He was convinced that his window of opportunity had closed. I was thrilled to tell him that the truth was far different.

IT'S NEVER TOO LATE TO DISCOVER YOUR ONE BIG THING

Raymond Chandler was one of America's greatest mystery writers. His classic stories about Detective Philip Marlowe have been read by millions, and multiple movies have been based on his books. His first novel, 1939's *The Big Sleep*, was made into a film starring Humphrey Bogart. He was also a writer for Paramount Pictures, and cowrote the screenplay for James M. Cain's brilliant novel, *Double Indemnity*.

But that all came late in life. In 1932, at forty-four years old, and at the midpoint of the Great Depression, Chandler was fired from his job. He was unemployed, some would say a philandering drunk, and at the end of his rope. Nonetheless, he and his wife decided to get away from all the failure and try to start over. Driving up the coast of California, Chandler randomly started reading a detective magazine, and the idea occurred to him that he could write stories like that.

He began by writing short detective stories in pulp magazines. These didn't pay well, but they gained him enough credibility to get a small book deal. He published his first novel at age fifty to only moderate success. After writing three more with still no great sales, he talked his publisher into allowing a smaller publisher to reprint his first book in paperback. To the shock of everyone involved, it sold three hundred thousand copies.

Raymond Chandler didn't discover his one thing until middle age, and yet he became one of the most popular and respected writers in his genre. His influence on subsequent writers and filmmakers has been enormous.

» Even after years in one direction, it may be time to change.

Around 1831, Samuel Morse was frustrated. He had given his life to be a painter—even traveled to Paris in pursuit of that dream. As historian David McCullough recounts in his book, *The Greater Journey*, painting had been Morse's dream since college and he had set his heart on that and that alone.

Years before his preacher father, Jedidiah Morse, had counseled him with the advice: "Attend to one thing at a time. The steady and undissipated attention to one object is the sure mark of a superior genius." As a result, Morse threw himself into painting, but after a series of setbacks he finally abandoned it. The crushing moment was his losing the appointment to paint a historic mural at the Capitol in Washington. With that lost, he gave up painting entirely.

As McCullough describes:

> He must attend to one thing at a time, his father had preached. The "one thing" henceforth would be his telegraph, the crude apparatus for which was also to be found in his New York University studio apartment. Later it would be surmised that had he not stopped painting when he did, no successful electromagnetic telegraph would have happened when it did, or at least not a Morse electromagnetic telegraph.[17]

Relatively late in his career, Samuel Morse gave up painting to focus on inventing the telegraph and eventually a language called Morse code, which literally changed the world.

ARE YOU HAULING ROCKS OR BUILDING A BETTER WORLD?

There's a brilliantly designed museum in Budapest dedicated to the Hungarian victims of terror who were starved, tortured, beaten, and killed first by the occupying Nazis in the early 1940s and then by the Soviets until 1956. The Terror House, as it's called, served as the headquarters for the security police of both sadistic regimes.

While shooting documentary film footage in Eastern Europe in 2011, Kathleen and I took the tour of the Terror House. It's one of the most fascinating examples of great design in a museum I've ever encountered. As we were walking through one of the galleries, I asked how the Soviets in particular could motivate so many people to build massive industrial projects—especially when it came to backbreaking labor—and work to the point of starvation.

The guide answered that years ago in Communist Russia a visitor happened upon a group of peasant workers clearing a field. It was tough work, hauling huge rocks, shoveling, and moving dirt by hand, all under the unmerciful heat of summer. The visitor noticed that while the workers were exhausted and some even seriously injured, they were all singing as they labored. They smiled—even in the midst of the pain and the grueling work.

He asked one of the workers, "How can you sing while hauling rocks?"

Without hesitation the worker replied, "Oh, we're not hauling rocks, we're building a better world."

When it comes to your life, what's your perspective? Are you hauling rocks or building a better world? In the day-to-day battle, it's often tough to see the bigger picture and learn the impact you're making in the world. But perspective matters.

Step back. Take the big view. Sure, you may be hauling rocks, but there's a bigger purpose behind it. It took thousands of nameless engineers and workers to build America's space program, and when a football team wins the Super Bowl, there are hundreds of people playing critical roles that are never featured on national television.

You may not be a leader and have no desire to become one. But discovering your OBT makes you more valuable to a team or a bigger effort. Great teams are built by knowing and exploiting each member's area of expertise, so to reach the next level in your career or calling, your OBT matters.

In other words, stop complaining about hauling rocks, and start celebrating your part in building a better world.

A BIG DIFFERENCE BETWEEN WINNERS AND LOSERS

The NBC television program, *The Office,* was originally built around a middle manager named Michael Scott who didn't have a clue when it came to personal awareness. Played brilliantly—now in syndication—by actor Steve Carrell (before he left the series in 2011), he doesn't get jokes, he's incredibly insensitive to the people around him, and he hasn't a clue about his own ability (that is, if he has any). The show is wildly popular and continues with new cast additions. The popularity and massive audience are a testimony to a character that viewers know all too well from their own experiences.

There are millions of Michael Scotts in the world.

Obviously, the discussion between what makes people winners or losers in life has been going on for thousands of years. I'm not especially big on the term *winners*, though, because it's difficult to calculate. What standard do you use? Some people die penniless but have lived incredible lives that impacted millions of people for the better. Most of the heroes who jumped in with both feet during the tragedy of 9/11 weren't financially successful, but in some cases gave their lives for their friends and fellow New Yorkers.

By the same token, there are plenty of billionaires whose lives have counted for very little when it comes to things that matter.

Yet one thing I've observed is people who live lives of significance aren't like Michael Scott at all—because they are people who truly know themselves. They can accurately tell you what their strengths and weaknesses are. They know where they need help, and where they need to grow. They have very few (if any) illusions when it comes to their expertise or potential. Most of all, they're remarkably humble about it all.

But there are a lot of Michael Scotts out there. I find they're way off base when it comes to their own lives; they're convinced they have talent where there is none, expertise that doesn't exist, and potential that no one else can see. They assert themselves in inappropriate places and take credit for work they didn't accomplish. That's why *The Office* has such resonance. We all know that cast of characters and, sadly, too many of us have worked for a Michael Scott.

In short, you can't make a difference in the world—and you won't find your OBT—if you don't have a clue about yourself. Comedy aside, the Michael Scotts have never taken the time to look deep into their own hearts; they've never taken a cold, hard, dispassionate look at who they are and what they're made of.

And they have no idea about their One Big Thing.

How about you? Have you taken that look lately? It's not too late.

Chapter Twelve

IT'S NOT ABOUT YOU

Living Out the Potential of Your One Big Thing

You can't manufacture passion or "motivate" people to feel passionate. You can only discover what ignites your passion and the passions of those around you.

—JIM COLLINS, FROM HIS BOOK *GOOD TO GREAT*

When your life is over, the world will ask you only one question: Did you do what you were supposed to do?

—KORCZAK ZIOLKOWSKI, POLISH-AMERICAN SCULPTOR OF THE CRAZY HORSE MEMORIAL

A few years ago while I was on a trip to London, the *London Times* newspaper reported that Malcolm Pearson—head of the United Kingdom's Independence Party, which advocates withdrawing Britain from the European Union—said he was stepping down.

In today's world of modern politics, another leader stepping down isn't unusual. I started to put down the paper and have another piece of toast. At least until I noticed his reason for resigning: "I'm terrible at this; I quit."

I had to hand it to him for his complete and unvarnished honesty; I wish more leaders understood themselves as well as Mr. Pearson. The old saying that quitters never win and winners never quit couldn't be more false, and in my opinion has resulted in far too many people spending their lives in pursuit of the wrong thing.

I'm an avid reader and have more than a thousand books in my library. I never go on a trip without a few books in my bag; I have a stack next to my desk of what I need to read next. But one thing reading so much has taught me is that if I start a book that isn't right for me, or isn't what I expected, I can put it down. No regrets, no guilt.

Perhaps I can give it to a friend who would enjoy it, or sell it in a garage sale. But if I don't like it, I get rid of it and move on. My wife isn't the same. Once she starts a book, no matter how painful, she'll finish. She has commitment, and likes to finish what she starts.

Some of us think holding on makes us strong; but sometimes it is letting go.
—Hermann Hesse, poet, novelist, and painter; winner of the Nobel Prize in Literature

There are millions of people in the workforce, in politics, in academics, and in the nonprofit world who are terrible at what they do. They're in over their heads and hopelessly lost.

The problem is they're terrified to admit it.

It's one thing to admit you're no good at snow skiing or scuba diving. But it's another thing entirely to admit you're no good at a job you've been doing for the last ten or more years. After all, you might be ridiculed.

A few years ago, I watched a friend and his wife go through an extraordinarily difficult divorce. They were both gifted in their fields, which happened to be exactly the same. But midway through their marriage, her career took off and his began to fall behind. The truth is, she was brilliant and deserved the success, but it left him embarrassed that he couldn't keep up.

Because of his upbringing, he could never reconcile himself to a wife who was more successful than him. Rather than celebrate with her, he sulked, and his frustration eventually turned into bitterness. It's one thing for your wife to be more successful than you, but—for some men—it's even worse when she's more successful at the same thing you do for a living.

Insecurity, fear, and inadequacy strangle the potential success for so many talented and gifted people. But that very insecurity and fear keep them from admitting it, and prevent them from searching for the place where they could find their OBT.

British politician Malcolm Pearson was reviled with critical newspaper coverage and became the brunt of jokes on the evening news throughout the UK. But admitting he was terrible at the job and taking responsibility for that generated a second wave of support. Once people had a moment to think about it, they wished everyone who truly stunk at his or her job had the courage to do the same.

I thought about putting the poor guy on a pedestal.

That old saying about quitters and winners is bunk. It's one thing to allow outside criticism, obstacles, or frustrations to stop you. I don't believe in that at all. But if you've gotten in over your head, don't know what you're doing, and things aren't going to change, then don't be afraid to step down. Allow a more qualified person to do the job. There's no harm in realizing your limitations. In fact, there's honor in it.

I'd like the "I'm terrible at this; I quit" T-shirt.

Let's start a movement.

» Are you good at your job, but not fulfilling your purpose?

Perhaps an even more difficult situation is that you've read this book and even though you're good at your job—perhaps even brilliant—you've also realized you're on the wrong path. You may have always suspected it, but now you know the truth.

You might even be an all-star at work. People respect you, and you've advanced through the company or at the university. You have awards on your wall and have contributed to your retirement fund. You have relationships in the community and responsibilities to your loved ones.

You have a job, a mortgage, a family.

But it's not fulfilling your purpose.

What do you do? Uproot, change everything, and step into the unknown, or turn away from what you know is the truth, and carry on as usual?

The question is—what sacrifice are you willing to make to fulfill your dream?

> **You are unlike anyone who has
> ever lived. But that uniqueness isn't
> a virtue, it's a responsibility.**
> —Mark Batterson, *Soulprint: Discovering
> Your Divine Destiny* (2011)

Before you jump ship and risk everything, let's consider a strategy for making that transition. My friend Alan Platt, a pastor and leadership expert from Pretoria, South Africa, gives a brilliant illustration of strategy:

You've signed up to participate in a 5K "fun run." The purpose is to raise money for a worthy charity and you've recruited your friends and family to participate for a great cause. You've worked out, showed up at the starting line with all the other runners, and are excited and ready to race.

The starter raises the gun and fires. But the racers look at the starter and ask, "What's the route?"

The starter shouts, "Go! Run!" But the racers look bewildered at which direction to go. The crowd is cheering, the sponsors are waving, but no one has any idea what to do next.

The big idea of the fun run is great. Easy to understand, and easy to get excited about. But it's the underlying details that become the problem.

Vision is what you want to accomplish. *Strategy* is how you get there.

Too many companies today have a great vision, with absolutely no idea how to accomplish that vision. And it's no different with our personal lives.

>> Even people who have discovered
their One Big Thing struggle
with how to make it happen.

Do I leave my current job?
Do I go back to school?
Do I work on the side?
Do I tell anyone?

While everyone is different, and in various stages of life, talent, and career, here are a few things to consider as you start refocusing your future on your one thing:

Be bold, but don't be dumb.

Begin today preparing, strategizing, and pursuing your purpose, but don't be drastic. No matter how noble your intentions, your dream will be thwarted if you're not in a position to make it happen. So don't quit the current job until you have a transition plan in place. I've met many men and women with great dreams, but absolutely no possibility of making those dreams happen because they cut off a lifeline—either quit their job too soon, alienated their families, or made other ill-conceived decisions. In their excitement to move forward into their purpose, they acted too quickly and it cost them money, stability, support, and sometimes the dream itself.

>> In our well-intended passion to
make things happen, we sometimes
become our own worst enemy.

In some cases, it might take time to transition into your dream on a full-time basis. Maybe you could start writing your book after hours, build a design portfolio on weekends, take night classes, or grow in your level of expertise. Plenty of successful authors keep a day job and build their writing career after everyone else has gone to bed (or in my case before anyone else gets up in the morning). Whatever your One Big Thing happens to be, chances are you can at least *begin* while you're in your current position.

Building your foundation is important, and there's plenty of preparation to do before you pull the trigger.

Don't burn your bridges.

When the time comes to make your transition, don't make enemies. If it's a case of leaving your day job, do it amicably and work hard to keep the relationship on good terms. Don't leave your boss in the lurch or your team holding the bag. Perhaps you could make the transition in stages and start by moving to a part-time basis. Offer to keep the relationship intact by freelancing or helping during their busy periods.

Either way you've created a potential fallback position when times get tough, helped with your financial transition, or, in some cases, recruited your first client. And never forget the power of a good recommendation. If your last employer won't recommend you or write you a good endorsement because the relationship ended badly, that's a real caution flag for future investors, clients, and employers.

More than anything, never forget that it's a small world out there, and chances are your boss or other team members know plenty of people in your industry. So especially if your plan is to launch into a similar business, you don't want them talking badly about you to potential clients or customers. Even on the rare chance that keeping the relationship intact means offering to wrap up your work on your own time or without pay, I'd consider it.

Leaving on good terms—even if it costs you financially in the short run—can reap a huge return down the road.

Trigger your connections.

In the age of social media, you have no excuse for not having a powerfully effective database of relationships and connections. When I was fired from my job in the Midwest at age thirty-six, the first freelance gig I landed was from an old friend who had left the same company just a couple of years before. That day I learned the power of relationships and from then on began tracking them more effectively.

I'm naturally friendly anyway and love meeting and engaging with people. So it's easy for me and I've deliberately focused a significant part of my career on the power of connections.

It's important to note that developing these relationships isn't about using people for your advantage. The connections should be genuine and honest. People can smell a con a mile away and you won't get very far pursuing people for selfish reasons. When meeting with people looking for advice, I can sense in the first minute if their motives are less than respectable. You've probably heard the old proverb, "People don't care how much you know until they know how much you care."

Believe it.

Keep your résumé polished.

I hope my own staff isn't reading this, but it never hurts to keep your résumé, demo reel, or portfolio up to date. We live in a volatile economy, and the lifelong employment that our parents enjoyed is a thing of the past. You never know when the opportunity to pursue your dream will happen, and it's not always about launching out on your own.

People who are conventionally clever get jobs on their qualifications (the past), and not on their desire to succeed (the future). Very simply, they get overtaken by those who continually strive to be better than they are.

—Paul Arden, author of *It's Not How Good You Are, It's How Good You Want to Be* (2003)

I love the attitude of freelancers working on film and television studio sets in Los Angeles. Freelancers go to bed every night out of a job and the next morning start looking again. At any given moment, they're only one gig away from living on the street. That's why they keep their contacts up to date, touch base regularly with past relationships, and never close the door on an opportunity. You can always tell a freelancer on the set because every time the director yells, "Cut!" they get on the phone looking for their next job.

Full-time employees, on the other hand, tend to take it easy and rely too much on the safety net of their salary and benefits package. They assume they'll always have the position, and it's not long before the outside relationships they knew fade, their résumé or demo reel gets out of date, and they close the door on outside possibilities.

As a result, if they're laid off, downsized, or fired, they're caught on their heels, unable to react in time. Further, I've noticed that the longer they're employed, the less likely they are to recognize the writing on the wall that indicates internal change coming. That's why so many employees get blindsided by layoffs and cutbacks.

You just don't see what you're not looking for.

Statistics from the Change Anything organization (change anything.com) confirm that premise: a whopping 87 percent of employees have been passed over for promotions or pay increases because they were unable to make the changes their bosses had requested.[18]

My advice? Treat your full-time job like a freelance position. Never close the door on change, and always be ready to shift gears or adapt to a new position. Keep the résumé ready, and never neglect the opportunity to expand your network and connect with people who can help take you from where you are to where you want to be.

Don't let an inability to see change coming make you extinct.

What can you do for someone else?

The faster you learn that it's not all about you the better off you'll be. I can't tell you the number of times I helped connect someone else to a job, only to have them come back weeks, months, or years later and extend me a similar favor. Help other people connect to their dream, and sooner or later, someone will help you connect to yours. I'm always on the lookout for attaching the right person to the right project. It becomes fun after awhile; seeing people land in the perfect position is an incredibly fulfilling feeling.

Will they always reciprocate? Not hardly. They'll be plenty of times when you'll help someone find the perfect position and he'll promptly forget all about you. One of the most baffling experiences I've had is helping people find jobs with some of our clients. In many cases, a client hires us to consult, and we quickly realize we need a good person on the inside of the organization to help make our ideas happen. So we spend enormous time helping the client find the right person and, in most cases, lead that person to a better position with a higher salary than he's ever had.

Then what does he do? Get rid of us. That's right. Baffling. After helping him land a great position, he turns around and convinces the client he doesn't need us anymore.

Human behavior is strange indeed.

So there's no question that your efforts to help others will sometimes not be returned, but that's not a reason to stop connecting people. The few that do make it more than worth it, and after all—it's the right thing to do.

And don't expect a piece of the action for making those connections. Making a percentage off a business deal for bringing certain parties to the table is normal business practice. But if you put your hand out waiting for a cut every time you connect someone then they'll eventually start avoiding you, and you'll end up in a worse place than before.

Finally, brace yourself for the risk.

Nothing is foolproof, and nothing is fair. The history of business is the story of individuals with a dream who risked it all for the power of an idea. Dreaming isn't "safe," and if you're looking for a sheltered, secure future, then your One Big Thing probably won't be it. The government can't provide a program to ensure your dream happens, there are no insurance policies to protect it, and no cushion to land on if you fail.

But discovering your OBT and then stepping out to pursue its reality will be the greatest adventure of your life. When that happens, work becomes passion, and you will join the ranks of the very few who have accepted the risk, calculated the peril, and leaped off the ledge.

Epilogue

YOU'RE NOT CRAZY

Here's to the crazy ones, the misfits, the rebels, the troublemakers, the round pegs in the square holes, the ones who see things differently. They're not fond of rules, and they have no respect for the status quo. You can quote them, disagree with them, glorify or vilify them. About the only thing you can't do is ignore them, because they change things. They push the human race forward, and while some may see them as the crazy ones, we see genius, because the people who are crazy enough to think they can change the world, are the ones who do.

—APPLE INC., "THINK DIFFERENT" COMMERCIAL (1997)

P ursuing your One Big Thing may be mistaken by your friends and family as losing your mind. In his book, *Spiritual Lives of the Great Composers*, Patrick Kavanaugh describes German-born composer Georg Friedrich Händel's composition of his *Messiah*. An unpredictable composer at best, Händel spent most of his up-and-down career relentlessly moving from one failure to another. In those days, the bankruptcy option didn't exist, and by 1741 he was overwhelmed with debt. Without a miracle, prison was obvious.

He decided to perform his farewell concert and retire a failure at age fifty-six. But when a friend, Karl Jennens, handed him a libretto based on selected Scriptures from the Bible, everything changed. As Kavanaugh describes, Händel threw himself into writing and in a staggering stretch completed part one in only six days, part two in only nine, and part three in another six. He worked feverishly, driven by one overwhelming purpose. Servants left meals outside the door, afraid to disturb him. Once, when a servant did find the courage to open the door, the startled composer cried out, with tears streaming down his face: "I did think I did see all Heaven before me, and the great God himself."

He had just finished what would become known as the "Hallelujah" chorus.

Händel completed an astounding 260 pages of orchestration in only twenty-four days. During that process, he didn't leave his house, and friends often found him sobbing with emotion. Considering the immensity of the work, some have considered it one of the greatest musical feats in history.

Messiah premiered in Dublin, Ireland, on April 13, 1742, for a charitable benefit that raised enough money to set free 142 men from debtor's prison. Poverty—the driving force that began the work—resulted in the freedom of others from the same fate.

A year later in London, the King of England attended a performance. As the first notes of the "Hallelujah" chorus began, he was so overwhelmed he rose to his feet, beginning a tradition that has continued for more than two hundred years. Its subsequent performances for charity did more to feed the hungry and transform the lives of the poor than any other single musical achievement.

Remarking about Händel in 1824, Beethoven said, "Händel was the greatest composer who ever lived. I would bare my head and kneel at his grave."

Throughout Händel's career, even his commercial successes were usually followed by financial disaster. He was attacked by the church and many at the time felt little reason to believe his talent was worthy of any kind of legacy—until *Messiah*. Händel had written many compositions over the years, but by far the one most people remember is that One Big Thing. Out of a past that was uneven at best, the creation of *Messiah* was a burst of creativity driven by the remarkable passion of a man who glimpsed his one real purpose.

It was as if he had been waiting his entire life for that moment.

**Good ideas come with a heavy burden,
which is why so few people execute
them. So few people can handle it.**
—Hugh MacLeod, artist (gapingvoid.com)

What is the moment you've been waiting for?

A life pursuing One Big Thing isn't easy, but it will settle your questions about why you're here and what you were born to do with your life. Helen Keller once said, "Life is either a great adventure or it's nothing."

Millions of people spend their lives in the pursuit of nothing, but you have chosen the great adventure.

Go. Seek it with everything you have, and don't look back.

ACKNOWLEDGMENTS

While it takes hundreds of solitary hours in front of a computer to write a book, it would never see the light of day without a team of remarkable people working very hard behind the scenes to make it happen. Starting with my always understanding agent, Rachelle Gardner, who is my writing champion; to Joel Miller and the incredibly supportive team at Thomas Nelson Publishers; publicist Jason Jones; and my brilliant book editor Jamie Chavez (who's taught me more about citations than my college English teacher).

The team at our production company, Cooke Pictures: Mandy Sellick (who protects my writing schedule with the tenacity of a guard dog), Matthew Koppin, Chandra Hope, and Brad Knull, who are creating the kinds of media projects I've always dreamed about producing.

Thanks to my long suffering wife, Kathleen, who, outside her million other roles, during the last six months helped lead our company, arranged our daughter's wedding, launched a new media organization, and managed a massive kitchen remodel, which gave me the time to research and write. None of this would be on paper without her.

Most of all, thanks to everyone who's ever come up to chat after one of my speaking engagements, book signings, or conferences. Your gracious questions and frustrations were the spark of this idea, and during my most difficult times at the keyboard, I would close my eyes, see your faces, and keep typing.

NOTES

1. Andrew Roberts, "History Books" (A Review), *The Wall Street Journal*, November 19, 2011.
2. Louise Story, "Anywhere the Eye Can See, It's Likely to See an Ad," *New York Times*, January 15, 2007, www.nytimes.com/2007/01/15/business/media/15everywhere.html.
3. Tim Mullaney, "Tech distractions for workers add up," *USA Today*, May 18, 2011, www.usatoday.com/tech/news/2011-05-18-social-media-worker-distractions_n.htm.
4. Matt Richtel, "Digital Overlaod: Your Brain on Gadgets," NPR, August 2, 2010, www.npr.org/templates/story/story.php?storyId=129384107.
5. "Quick Facts About Nonprofits," National Center for Charitable Statistics, nccs.urban.org/statistics/quickfacts.cfm.
6. "Internet 2010 in numbers," Pingdom blog, January 12, 2011, royal.pingdom.com/2011/01/12/internet-2010-in-numbers/.
7. "New Book Titles and Editions, 2002–2010," R. R. Bowker, www.bowkerinfo.com/pubtrack/AnnualBookProduction2010/ISBN_Output 2002-2010.pdf .
8. Ross Luippold, "The Most Ridiculous Magazines of All Time," Huffington Post, May 25, 2011, www.huffingtonpost.com /2010/09/09/ridiculous-magazines_n_710942. html#s136454&title=Model_Airplane_News.
9. Tim Gautreaux, "A Conversation with Tim Gautreaux," *Image*, Number 63, Fall 2009, p 46.
10. William Grimes, "Geroge Lang, Mastermind Behind Café des Artistes, Dies at 86," *New York Times*, July 6, 2011, www.nytimes.com/2011/07/07/nyregion/george-lang-of-cafe-des-artistes-dies-at-86.html?pagewanted=all (accessed 29 November 2011).
11. Taped interview with George Lang, CBS Sunday Morning, July 10, 2011.

12. Rachel Dodes, "The Hit No One Wanted," *Wall Street Journal*, July 15, 2011, online.wsj.com/article/SB10001424052702304911104576444453903049990.html?mod=WSJ_ArtsEnt _LifestyleArtEnt_4.

13. Seth Doane, "Cities on the rise like never before," CBS News, May 22, 2011, www.cbsnews.com/video/watch/?id=7366882n&tag=mncol;lst;1.

14. Michael Greger, MD, "Appendix 25—Medspeak," United Progressive Alumni, upalumni.org/medschool/appendices /appendix-25.html.

15. L. P. Rowland, letter to the *New England Journal of Medicine*, 301(1979):507.

16. Geoff Mulgan, "Beware the jargon in academic-speak," Times Higher Education, December 13, 1996, www.timeshighereducation .co.uk/story.asp?storyCode=91656&sectioncode=26.

17. David McCullough, *The Greater Journey: Americans in Paris* (New York: Simon & Schuster, 2011).

18. K. Patterson, J. Grenny, D. Maxfield, R. McMillan, and A. Switzer, *Change Anything: The New Science of Personal Success* (New York: Business Plus, 2011).

ABOUT THE AUTHOR

An internationally known writer and speaker, Phil Cooke has also written *Jolt!: Get the Jump on a World That's Constantly Changing*, about how to make today's culture of disruption and change work for you, and *Branding Faith: Why Some Churches and Non-Profits Impact the Culture and Others Don't*, which forever changed the way nonprofit and religious organizations use the media to tell their story.

Through his media production and branding company (Cooke Pictures in Burbank, California), he's helped some of the largest nonprofit organizations and leaders in the world tell their stories in a distracted and disrupted culture. Cooke has lectured at many universities, including Yale, University of California at Berkeley, and UCLA, and blogs for the *Huffington Post*. At his own blog at philcooke.com he writes daily about the intersection of media, culture, and faith.

Cooke lives in Burbank, California, with his wife, Kathleen.

INDEX